SO-AZF-238

Alcohol and the Church

Alcohol and the Church

Developing an Effective Ministry

by
Margaret A. Fuad

Hope Publishing House
Pasadena, California

Copyright © 1992 Hope Publishing House

All rights reserved.

Hope Publishing House
Southern California Ecumenical Council
696 South Madison Avenue
Pasadena, California 91106 - U.S.A.
Telephone: (818) 792-6123; FAX (818) 792-2121

Thanks is due the following publishers and authors for their generous permission to quote from the following: *Alcoholics Anonymous,* Third Edition, 1976, by Alcoholics Anonymous World Services, Inc. *A Biblical Perspective on the Use and Abuse of Alcohol and Other Drugs,* by T. Furman Hewitt. *Alcohol and Substance Abuse,* by Stephen P. Apthorp. "The Bottom Line," address by Ernest P. Noble, by ARIS, publishers. The *Constitution,* the *Book of Confessions* and the *Book of Order* of the Presbyterian Church (U.S.A.), by the Office of the General Assembly. *Dying for a Drink,* by Anderson Spickard, M.D. and Barbara R. Thompson. *The New Strong's Exhaustive Concordance of the Bible,* James Strong, by Thomas Nelson, publishers. *Sober Life,* by John H. Spahr. *Understanding and Counselling the Alcoholic,* by Howard J. Clinebell. Permission to appropriate specific ideas by indirect quotation is given for the following: *Drinking: A Christian Position,* by Arnold B. Come and *Stumbling Blocks or Stepping Stones,* by Karl L. Schneider. All Scriptural references and quotations are from the New English Bible, 1971, unless otherwise indicated. Names have been changed to protect the privacy of various individuals whose stories are told herein.

Cover design - Christina Rodriguez
Printed in the U.S.A. on acid-free paper
Distributed by Spring Arbor Distributors

Library of Congress Cataloging-in-Publication Data

Fuad, Margaret A.
      Alcohol and the church : developing an effective ministry / Margaret A. Fuad.
            p.   cm.
      Includes index and bibliographical references.
      ISBN 0-932727-51-4 -- ISBN 0-932727-50-6 (pbk.)
      1. Church work with alcoholics. 2. Drinking in the Bible. 3. Wine--Biblical teaching. I. Title.
      BV4460.5.583   1992
      261.8'32292-DC20   91-42493
                                                              CIP

To Carol

Acknowledgments ❖

Although this book was actually written with my own pen in my own hand, it would never have come together between these covers without the inspiration, help and support of many folks. First, I thank my husband, Hilmi, whose strong encouragement, patience and generosity never flagged; and my son and daughter-in-law, Peter and Barbara who are thrilled to have a book in the family.

In preparation for this work—although we didn't know it at the time—my appreciation goes to Frank and Sherline Ross, my first mentors in the field of alcoholism; to the many persons who gave their firm support and loyalty as we linked arms in the early days of the Presbyterian Alcohol Network, particularly William B. Ailes, Dean H. Lewis, Paul Koper and wife, David C. Hancock, C. Howard Wallace, and Frank K. McDowell—all persons of the cloth; and similarly, I thank the patient congregation of my beloved First Presbyterian Church in Visalia, California, and the Presbytery of San Joaquin both among whom I promoted programs of alcohol ministry. Lastly, my love and gratitude go to those whose stories I have told in this book.

Then as I wrote, I am grateful for the encouragement and prayers of all with whom I discussed it, of those who read the original manuscript, and especially of my dear friends in the "6:30 A.M." study group who endured with me, and of Dorothy Coffman who assisted in school-teacherly fashion with the Syllabus.

For the no small task of skillful editing and bringing my writing to fruition, I thank Faith A. Sand of Hope Publishing House—and before that thanks to Roland W. Tapp, my first editor who encouraged me to go ahead with this needed challenge to the churches.

Finally, through all and in all, I thank God for the rich experience this writing has been and for keeping me at it until its completion! May you, the readers, find such blessing.

Table of Contents ❖

Throughout this book, *alcoholism* is considered a chronic, primary and hereditary disease characterized by repetitive drinking and loss of control over imbibing alcoholic beverages which results in deleterious physical, mental, social and economic problems to the drinker, family and close associates.

Introduction ❖

This book, which has grown out of my own experience, is written to help fill a gap in the literature which deals with alcoholism and other alcohol-related problems. The gap, more like a canyon, encompasses the lack of information plus the failure to challenge and provide how-to geared toward the religious community on methods they can use to meet the crying need of individuals and families in the church population and surrounding communities whose lives are miserably entangled in alcoholism and alcohol misuse.

It is my hope that the faint echoes now reverberating in this canyon will become great shouts of joy from those released from their suffering because they have encountered people of God who cared and acted to help them in their distress. Not only an atmosphere of empathy is needed in the church, but the religious community must be challenged toward zeal for this mission. I have arrived at this point in my pilgrimage convinced that God has been directing and challenging me along the way.

The great ends of the church are the proclamation of the gospel for the salvation of humankind: the shelter, nurture and spiritual fellowship of the children of God: the maintenance of divine worship; the preservation of the truth; the promotion of social righteousness; and the exhibition of the kingdom of heaven to the world.[1]

The church and its mission is something I know about, for I have spent my life in it. Born into a Christian home, I cannot recall my life without a personal relationship with Jesus Christ. Even during dark days, I have always known the security of this relationship. I was also born with an organizational manual in my hand. (I have frequently wished it had been a silver spoon in my mouth instead!)

Early on I loved working in and through the church, always trying to keep in mind that the earthly organization was a means to carry out the Great Commission of Matthew 28:19: preaching the gospel, providing nurture and fellowship for believers, and reaching out with a helping hand to those in need that all might find fullness of life in every way.

I planned and studied through college and two years of seminary to become a foreign missionary, but World War II prevented me from going overseas. Instead, for a few years I worked as a Christian education director and continued as a volunteer in that field after my marriage.

---

[1] Book of Order, *The Constitution of the Presbyterian Church (U.S.A.),* (New York: Office of the General Assembly, 1981) Sec. G-1.0200.

During these same years I was active in the women's organization of the church. After some 35 years (I began at age 15) of teaching and leadership with children and youth, I relinquished that ministry and found new activity in the church's adult education arena and in community service involving mental health, farm labor, hunger, housing, minority rights, and finally, alcohol problems.

In 1968 my election as the first woman elder in our local Presbyterian church opened up a wide new vista of involvement, culminating in election to the board of the Program Agency of the General Assembly (national level) of the United Presbyterian church. This gave me a chance to get an even broader overview of how the church is involved in helping people around the world.

An interest in alcohol problems also began early in my career. When I was twelve, a little, bird-like lady in her "golden-years" gathered together a few of us fledglings from the Sunday school in order to broaden our education on some life issues. Prohibition was yet in effect, but she was determined that we understand the effect of drinking alcoholic beverages.

I will never forget the scrap of brain tissue preserved in a jar she brought to class. Dangling this awesome specimen in our faces she proceeded to explain how alcohol affected first the top of the brain, lowering one's inhibitions. As more was imbibed, drunkenness with its attendant dangers and sorrows overtook.[2] I was converted

---

[2] This is still generally accepted, as increased research is being done on the effects of alcohol on the brain.

on the spot and decided that I was not going to jeopardize *my* brain functions.

It was not so simple for my sister, five years my junior. A bright, pretty and active young woman, she trained as a nurse and became one of the first commercial airline stewardesses. This led to her volunteering as an army flight nurse in World War II—a difficult duty, flying the wounded back from Europe in those slow tubs (it now seems) of planes without sufficient oxygen and tense with concern for her charges. It was in the army she really learned to drink.

After the war ended, Carol married her army sweetheart and while he finished his education and began his career, she set up house and had babies. The jolt came 14 years into their marriage when their fifth child was born after a difficult pregnancy and delivery. Her drinking was finally recognized as a problem. The baby went home from the hospital with a housekeeper-nurse. My sister went to an alcoholism recovery center.

To say our families were shocked is an understatement. We were totally ignorant about alcoholism, its signs, or what it took to get over it! However, to our credit, none of us turned against her but instead rallied around, praying for her family and eventually welcoming her home with joy. She became an avid AA (Alcoholics Anonymous) member and enjoyed 16 years of sobriety before her death. To her memory I dedicate this book.

A decade after that familial trauma a psychiatrist, knowledgeable about alcohol and other drugs, became the head of our local mental health services. In an effort to do something about the burgeoning drug and alcohol problems in our county, he called a meeting which I attended. Within a week I was elected chair of a task force charged with establishing a much needed half-way house for alcoholics. Some two dozen enthusiastic people joined together and did it!

On that night when I agreed to chair the task force, I felt God's hand on me, directing me in this ministry. My experience in the church enabled me to furnish the necessary leadership to the task force so together we could accomplish the goal. Along with raising money and doing all sorts of sometimes odd tasks, I studied and learned all I could about alcoholism and alcohol-related problems. With a measure of surprise, to be sure, I learned that misuse of alcohol and alcoholism have a spiritual basis, and that recovery from alcoholism is definitely a spiritual enterprise.

Eventually I began to wonder why the church, my first love, appeared to ignore such a pervasive problem. When I went on the board of the Program Agency, I began to work on this discrepancy at the national level. From those efforts was born the Presbyterian Alcohol Network (now the Presbyterian Network on Alcohol and Other Drug Abuse) which has reached hundreds within the Presbyterian community and stimulated significant action.

I became founding editor of the *Alcohol Network News,* the organization's newsletter sent to those in the church who were concerned about alcohol problems and thought the church should be dealing with them. During those years, I corresponded with myriads of readers who either wanted to know how they could participate in such a ministry or who wanted to share news of their successful programs.

During this experience I discovered the paucity of helpful tools available to those in the church working with alcoholism. Finally, it seemed that I needed to do what I have repeatedly done through the years—seeing a need I stepped in. So I now take pen in hand to organize the lessons I have learned and pass on suggestions made by many about how the church needs to work in this challenging field.

This is a message for both laity and clergy, challenging all to work together. I offer a special challenge to lay persons because this ministry needs, indeed demands, talents plus time which many lay-persons can give more readily. But whoever is there, reading this book, I pray you will do it!

PART I

THE CHURCH SHOULD ❖

1

The Need ❖

Then he called his twelve disciples to him and gave them authority to cast out unclean spirits and to cure every kind of ailment and disease (Mt 10:1).

We sat in a pastor's quiet study. "How did you find your sobriety?" a member of our newly organized Alcohol Awareness Committee of the Presbytery asked Dorene during our time of sharing.

After hesitating a minute at the unusually direct question, Dorene told her story. "Early one morning I woke up on the floor of my apartment and saw the young minister of the Presbyterian Church in the next town on his knees, praying over me. In that instant in my dim, bleary, drunken consciousness, something happened! Somebody really cared and had put himself out for me!

Somebody answered his prayer for me—God! Lying on

that floor I suddenly became somebody who mattered! With Kevin's help, I got up, staggered dizzily to a chair and drank some of the coffee he had made. Later that day, he sent an AA member to invite me to a meeting. With the help of Kevin, that AA member who became my sponsor and the AA group, I got through those first difficult days and weeks of learning to live without booze. Now here I am, nine years later, sober and wanting to help others as I was helped."

"How come the pastor knew about you?" asked another committee member.

"I really don't know," replied Dorene. "I had attended the church a few times and liked it because it was small and the people were friendly. Also, it was not my own denomination where somebody might know me. See, I'd been in the church all my life; really believed in God and in Christ; taught Sunday school; was president of the women's league; and all kinds of things. I drank secretly for a long time, but inevitably I went public. After having been stopped several times for drunk driving and taken home by the officer, I was finally arrested and jailed. I was so shaken and remorseful after *that* night that I thought I surely must resign from all my church activities and withdraw from the church. When I told my pastor what I was going to do, he said, kindly, 'No, don't do that. We won't say anything about it—you just try to do better.' Little did he know!

"I couldn't stop drinking. I became so disgusted with myself. My marriage broke up and I lost my children. I was completely discouraged and wanted to die." After a pause while she looked out the window, Dorene continued. "Somewhere, not too long after that time, I heard that alcoholism was a disease. Maybe there was hope after all, I thought in a fleeting moment of clarity: diseases could be cured. Of course, being alone, I had to work, so I took a job as a bookkeeper in the town next to Kevin's parish. Only God knew why I had to move so far away from my previous home, for I didn't find real help and sobriety until Kevin recognized what ailed me and took time to help me.

᷿ ᷿ ᷿

Now at the Sheep Pool in Jerusalem there is a place with five colonnades. Its name in the language of the Jews is Bethesda. In these colonnades there lay a crowd of sick people, blind, lame and paralysed. Among them was a man who had been crippled for 38 years. When Jesus saw him lying there and was aware that he had been ill a long time, he asked him: "Do you want to recover?," "Sir," he replied, "I have no one to put me in the pool when the water is disturbed, but while I am moving someone else is in the pool before me." Jesus answered, "Rise to your feet, take up your bed and walk." The man recovered instantly, took up his stretcher and began to walk (Jn 5:2-9).

Dave was at that same meeting of our Awareness Committee, quiet and tentative. He had been urged to join us by his observant pastor who long had wanted something done in the Presbytery in the way of ministry with alcohol problems. On a Sunday morning two years later some of us heard his story as he told it unselfconsciously to a class in one of the churches where we were conducting an alcohol educational series.

During his early teens Dave, now 27, recounted how he learned to drink with the other kids—chiefly beer. Not too much trouble occurred, however, until he acquired that beloved symbol of growing-up—a driver's license. Then came citations and arrests when he might be taken home from the precinct by a family member.

Amazingly, nobody tumbled to why he was having so much trouble with the law. Even Dave didn't. Finally one of those late nights after the tavern had closed he collided with another car. Thankfully no one was injured, but Dave was very drunk. He was taken to the drunk tank of the jail in the nearby county where the accident had occurred. In the morning, when he was charged, he realized that he was probably due for a stay in that notoriously wretched jail.

He was bailed out by his distraught wife, but while riding home he decided that he just could not go to that jail. In his misery, a thought began to take shape in his aching head: he had been thrown in the drunk tank, could beer be the problem? He admitted it did make him drunk! For the first time in his life he thought that his life was out of control and useless.

Thoughts of ending it weighed heavily on him. Just then he remembered an older man, Bob, who had long been the "town drunk" but who now had been sober for several years. He even had offered publicly to help anyone who wanted help. Dave telephoned Bob and asked if he would help him—what could he lose by asking? In a cheerful voice, Bob said that he would meet him in a half-hour at that new coffee shop on the edge of town.

As they sat across from each other in a booth with coffee, Bob explained how he had finally been able to give up drinking and assured Dave that he could do likewise through the strength of Jesus Christ.

Was it so? Dave didn't know, but this man had something he wanted—peace and a joy in living. With tears dropping into his coffee cup, Dave prayed, repeating the words after Bob, "Jesus please save me, I need you." His simple petition was answered, and he was miraculously born to a new life.

It wasn't easy at first. At times the temptations were overwhelming and giving in was easier that fighting. However, as time went by and his faith in Jesus Christ grew, so did his ability to stand up against the temptations. He joined the Presbyterian church in his town after he discovered the understanding pastor, and there he has made many supportive friends and been elected to office. Study of the Bible in groups or alone is a daily fascination, prayer a daily strength. The passage from John 5, cited above, is one of his favorites. Like the lame man who could never quite reach the healing pool, he feels Christ came and lifted him and put him on his feet again.

❧ ❧ ❧

Cast your burden on the Lord, and he will sustain you (Ps 55:22).

Then there was Jean, a faithful member of our

Awareness Committee from the beginning who had attended my church occasionally a year before we organized the committee. I had met her briefly at church and then had bumped into her once when I dropped by the local agency of the National Office on Alcoholism to get a few pamphlets. At my urging she came back to church the next Sunday and soon she and her three lively and pretty teenage daughters joined the church and took active part in several activities. We became good friends.

Early in our friendship, Jean explained forthrightly that she was a recovering alcoholic. She had been psychologically addicted,[3] she said, and had gone through the program in the recovery center I had helped start, finding sobriety and also meeting Rudy. Eventually they were married in our church in a simple but heartfelt ceremony. Jean has continued sober year after year, in spite of ups and downs, living daily in deepening faith and trust in God as she attends AA, Al-Anon and church.

For Rudy, it was not so easy. Approaching 40 years of age when we first met, he had experienced more trouble and pain than most people who have lived twice as long. Born into an alcoholic family, turned out early to fend for himself and with his own drinking problem, he found himself married, divorced and married several more times while in his cups, in spite of not having always been properly released from the previous marriage.

As a result of these entanglements, he served eight

---

[3] James E. Royce, *Alcohol Problems and Alcoholism* (New York: The Free Press, 1981) p. 88.

horrendous years in a state prison. After being released, he came to his grandmother in California, found a job in the railroad yards, married a young woman named Betty—legally and happily. Because of Betty's faithfulness in her Christian life, he was about to join her church, when tragically she and their new baby were killed when her automobile was hit by a locomotive pulling a train of freight cars which Rudy had supervised putting together! In his wild and persistent grief, he blamed God for the tragedy. His drinking, which had abated, began again in earnest.

Eventually, he arrived at the recovery center in our town, determined to sober up. He made good progress and soon was counselling others in the home. After he and Jean were married, life was good for awhile as they built up a maintenance business which supported them and the children well. But the stress was too much, it seemed, and Rudy slipped back into drinking.

After a few weeks he was allowed to return to the recovery center, but slipped again after leaving the facility. While pigging out on beer, he had a severe heart attack. Fortunately he was near a hospital where he was revived with much chest-thumping and injections.

As he lay there in bed, amazed to be alive but filled with remorse, our young associate pastor visited him. After talking and reading from the Bible, the pastor prayed for Rudy's healing. During the prayer, as Rudy told it, a great euphoria lifted him and before the "Amen" was said, he gasped, "I feel really clean, really forgiven for the first time." A month later he joyously confessed Christ as Lord as he was baptized and joined our church which he attended faithfully.

However as the months passed, stresses in his work and now in his marriage began to mount and Rudy, shifting into automatic, was again in relapse. I missed Rudy at church the next Sunday and unaware of what had happened, I asked Jean about him. Hollow-eyed and with quavering voice, she told me that she had reached the end of her rope and had sent Rudy packing.

What to think and what to do about it were the questions in our minds. Quietly Jean and I agreed between us that we must give Rudy into God's hands as literally and completely as we could. We bowed our heads there, standing in front of the church after Sunday service when almost everyone had gone home, and simply told God that we were powerless, we could do no more, we could worry no more—and to please take and care for Rudy wholly.

Later, after a short reconciliation with Jean and a seemingly serious spate of church attending and AA meetings, Rudy fell off the wagon once more and left home. A few weeks later he telephoned Jean for a short, cryptic conversation. An hour later a friend discovered him dead of a heart attack. The coroner said that every organ in his body was damaged irreparably by alcohol.

In faith, Jean and I believe that Rudy now is really in God's hands and at peace at last.

These are the stories—in part—of four recovering alcoholics intermingled in my life and the lives of the churches of which they are a part. I could tell you of many more, but I mention them to illustrate a point. Perhaps you know some equally afflicted and courageous people, but chances are good that you may not. Our society and our churches do not make such friendships easily possible yet I am convinced that as serious Christians and church members we must find a way to make such friendships and concerns possible through our personal and group ministries.

2

Reaching Out ❖

"I say to you, stand up. Take your bed and go home."
And he got up, took his stretcher at once and went out
in full view of them all, so that they were astounded
and praised God. "Never before," they said, "have we
seen the like!" (Mk 2:11,12).

This gospel account was written by that energetic young man, Mark, who wrote down the Apostle Peter's recollection of Jesus as he went about with his disciples during his ministry on earth. Bothering little with chronology, Mark records these reminiscences so that he reveals Jesus as the son of God who speaks with authority, is without fear, but is filled with tender love and willingness to pay attention to needs of individual people in the throngs who gathered around him.

When this narrative begins (Mk 2:1) Jesus is at home

after several days of going around to neighboring towns, but there is no rest for him. The word of his preaching and healing had spread like wildfire among the people who were hungering for a liberating contact with God and searching for wellness in a day when medical help as we know it was unavailable. At the crack of dawn, they begin to come to see and hear him, jostling each other in the courtyard, trying to get through the gateway and milling about in the narrow dusty street.

On the edge of the crowd four men appear carrying a paralyzed friend on a stretcher. With much elbowing and remonstrance they get near Jesus' house. The crowd is solid. How do they get inside where Jesus is? One man bends over to the others and murmurs, "Let's go up to the roof and see if we can get him in from up there."

With more bumping and shoving, the poor man on the stretcher holding on as best he can, they make it up the outside stairs. Removing some roof tiles, they uncover a hole large enough to let him down with ropes, right in front of Jesus!

What a feat—and how taken aback everyone is! When Jesus sees the four peering down at him he recognizes their faith and says to the invalid, "My son, your sins are forgiven" (Mk 2:5).

Before the man can react to what Jesus had said, some lawyers (scribes) who were sitting there question in their minds about this "fellow's" authority to forgive sins. Surely what he had just said was total blasphemy!

Jesus reading their thoughts, asks them which is easier to say, "Your sins are forgiven," or "Stand up, take your bed and walk?" To convince them, he turns to the paralyzed man and says just that: "Stand up, take your bed and go home." The man in joy, gets up, tucks his stretcher under his arm and as the astounded people open a path for him, he goes out.

Through the ages people have flocked to listen when the gospel is proclaimed in power and truth. People yearn for a word from God—however they may conceive of God—which will give meaning to their lives, hope for the future and healing to their souls and bodies. The crowds in their eagerness sometimes block access to the messenger—Christ—so that desperately needy persons cannot get through to hear, see or touch Christ—or be touched by him.

Nevertheless, the good news is that interested and determined friends can clear the way to Christ for these persons so that healing of body and soul can take place. A complete theological understanding of this healing process is not essential—only faith and obedience are required.

ᔕ ᔕ ᔕ

We can learn some effective guidelines by trying to re-read this gospel story through an alcoholic's reddened, despairing eyes—or the tearful eyes of family members—or through the fearful eyes of victims of other alcohol abuse.

The crowd outside the house where Jesus was speaking, if it were representative of a crosscut of society today, would include some alcoholics, their families, friends and others devastated by misuse of alcohol. We do not know much of how the populace was affected by alcohol-related problems in Jesus' day, but we do know that at present in the United States, of persons who drink (about 70 percent of the adult population) 1.2 million people have one or more symptoms of alcoholism. Beyond this, four others close to each one of these persons is affected adversely. Adding to this total of six million people, the estimated ten million who are chronic alcohol abusers (but not alcoholics) plus those whose lives are affected by this group, we now confront a quarter of our society.

Some of these alcohol-buffeted people are bound to be in every crowd, especially one made up of people looking for help like those who came to see Jesus. Through our new alcohol-reflected eyes, we see the crowd in yet another way—a phalanx of bodies barring the overlooked and unseemly sufferer from getting near Christ and his liberating and healing message. And so today a phalanx of "programs" often keeps the average congregation so busy with promoting and using up their time, energy and talents that suffering persons are slighted.

All churches prioritize their concerns. Beyond the virtually mandatory services of worship with preaching, evangelism, observance of the Sacraments, church-school, Bible study, prayer, fellowship and official meetings, there are others elected from many fields of concern: abortion, disaster relief, family life, ecology, faith and politics, criminal and economic justice, health, housing, human rights, hunger, missions overseas, life-style, peacemaking, personal growth and racial problems—to name a few.[4]

In no way would I imply that these programs in themselves are questionable or should be done away with. They are all imperative for the maintenance and strengthening of our faith in obedience as we carry out the biblical mandate to share our beliefs in every aspect of life (Jm 1:22). I have spent much of my time and energy in the "mandatory" programs and several of the elective ones throughout my life, but I have also been convinced of my call of God to reach out in ministry to those affected by alcohol problems. In the process I have seen that it is easy for us in the church community to become so enveloped in these programs that our vision becomes myopic and our very energies so sapped that crucial needs, often on our doorsteps, are ignored and overlooked as our attention is diverted.

I speak from painful experience. How could I have been so ignorant when one of these crucial problems—alcoholism—struck in my own family? When the opportunity came to do something about it in my community, I discovered I knew virtually nothing about this problem. I began to ask myself why, having been seriously committed to so many of the church programs mentioned above, had I never heard that alcoholism is the number one

---

[4] These are selected from the alphabetical "Table of Contents" of the *Resource Guide for Church Leaders* (New York: Presbyterian Church [U.S.A.] 1984). They represent about one-third of the programs for which literature and other helps are available. (There is a short section on alcohol abuse there largely at the insistence of the Presbyterian Alcohol Network.) Most major denominations have similar lists of helps.

health problem in our nation, ranks third in mortality and first in morbidity. Neither did I know that alcohol is the great facilitator in 80 percent of all crime, e.g., child and spouse abuse, rape, homicides, assaults, arson; that it is a significant factor in poverty, divorce, runaways and suicides; that there are 28 million children (both juvenile and adult) of alcoholic parents with deep emotional problems; that it is a causative factor in 25,000 traffic deaths yearly; taking a vast cumulative toll in human lives and decent living. Beyond this, for the society at large it costs a huge sum ($136.3 billion in 1990) to pick up the pieces of the relentless fallout from alcohol-related misery.

And why, when alcoholism struck my family, had I never, in thousands of sermons, talks and studies with "spiritual" emphases, heard that alcohol problems have a definite spiritual dimension? God forgive me—us!

Looking again at the crowd in our story, we see another possible gathering, one of invisibles, which effectively precludes those who are sick and tired of being sick and tired from finding release from drinking problems. These ghostly beings are the myths which frequently crowd out those who need help and those who might help them. Following are some which may well be in this eerie crowd:

1. Nothing can be done about alcohol—it's here to stay; besides Prohibition was a failure.
2. Temperance, that means abstinence. Count me out.
3. It's a personal matter, so we shouldn't get involved.
4. Alcoholic beverages are part of the good American life. So be it.

5. Doing something about alcohol problems, e.g., taxes or advertising, would interfere with profits or even free speech.
6. Only experts can help.
7. All that's needed to quit drinking too much is will-power.
8. Let AA do it.
9. The alcoholic must hit bottom before he can be helped.
10. Get rid of the alcoholic and the family will be OK.
11. We don't have any alcohol problems in our church.
12. We don't want messy people like that around our children.
13. The French drink lots of wine and they do all right.

Myths are just that—mythical: "fabricated, invented, or imagined in . . . defiance of the facts," my dictionary says.[5] In spite of our knowing this, we tend often to accept such myths as fact. But these familiar bromides stand in the way of the church community reaching out to heal.

Gratefully, another thing occurs as we read this Bible story through the eyes of alcohol misusers—or their victims. There is a happy ending for at least one very ill person who got through to Jesus. Interestingly, the King James Version says the invalid in this story "was sick of the palsy" (v. 3) which is defined by the dictionary[6] as "paralysis, a condition marked by uncontrollable tremor

---

[5] *Webster's Seventh New Collegiate Dictionary* (Springfield, MA: G. and C. Merriam Co. 1967) p. 561.
[6] op. cit., p. 607.

of the body." Could this man have had the "shakes" of an alcoholic sobering-up? It is a helpful exercise, in any case, to think of an alcoholic lying on that stretcher.

This fortunate invalid made it to Jesus and was healed because four devoted friends were willing to carry him laboriously and, with ingenuity, deposit him in front of Christ. The carriers must have been genuinely concerned people who were willing to go to great trouble to get help for their ill friend. Just think, if there had been no one to intercede for him, this man's situation would have been dire. Caring friends made the difference between being healed or remaining ill and a slave to sin.

Or maybe these four weren't mere friends, but rather relatives who were the ones most affected by his sad state. Maybe they were brothers, cousins or even his father. Whoever they were, they cared enough and were bold enough to do what they could to get help for him despite the problems he gave them, or the logistics of getting that help.

In fact, could we not consider this band of helpers the ancient forerunners of AA members doing "Twelfth-step Work"?[7] They knew that the only real recovery for their friend—from alcoholism or whatever his "palsy" meant— had to be spiritually motivated. And when this Jesus

---

[7] See Appendix for list of the Twelve Steps of Alcoholics Anonymous. "Twelfth Step Work" consists of visits or other encounters by recovering AA members with an alcoholic who is still drinking and who is possibly seeking help. The recovering persons share their story of finding sobriety and, if the alcoholic demonstrates a will to accept help, they shepherd the newly recovering person in the early days of recovery and attendance at AA meetings.

spoke with authority about the Kingdom of God, they had found success!

So, continuing to read this gospel story through our borrowed eyes, we find the excitement increasing. When Jesus saw the faith not only of the paralyzed man but also that of his expectant friends, he said promptly, "My son, your sins are forgiven!"

Heads turned. Glances were exchanged. Bystanders murmured, "What a strange thing to say!" Even his friends may have muttered, "Really, we just wanted his paralysis taken away." It is easy to react just that way when we encounter similar persons. But Jesus goes deeper than just the outward sign of his inward malady.

After deftly answering the lawyers who questioned his presumptuous statement which they regarded as heretical, Jesus healed the man physically as well. In joyful obedience he folded up his bed and walked home— quite a feat for a paralytic who was weak or stiff from years of inaction!

The physical healing was the overt, visible event for which the crowd cheered as they praised God. They couldn't perceive as obviously, nor understand how important the forgiving of the man's sins was to him or his friends and family. They were probably like us—slow to grasp the significance in the face of the immediate joy of the physical healing. Only later did it finally dawn that a great load of enervating guilt had been lifted from the healed man's spirit and he was freed to have a new and living relationship with God. He was transformed, both physically and spiritually!

❧ ❧ ❧

To recovering alcoholics, as well as their family and friends, this gospel story illustrates the recovery process from alcoholism. The imprisoned spirit must be liberated as the bodily addiction is healed to ensure a new, sober life. The founders of Alcoholics Anonymous, Bill W. and Dr. Bob, articulated this truth. (It was like Columbus discovering America—it was there all the time, but nobody had dared make the trip!)

The not-so-secret secret of AA is that recovery of both aspects of being—the physical and the spiritual—begin simultaneously and continue as the alcoholics surrender daily in faith and obedience to the restorative and sustaining power of God, as they understand God. The same can be said for those "significant others" who suffer along with the alcoholic who is in their midst as well as for those who misuse alcohol in other ways.

Dr. Howard J. Clinebell, Jr., writes about this miracle in his basic book on pastoral counselling with alcoholics:

The genius of Protestantism has been its emphasis on what is described in biblical language as "salvation by grace through faith." This is essentially the experience of acceptance. Through a religious experience the person feels accepted by God. He does not earn this acceptance. It is his because he is a child of God. When he comes to the place in his own experience, often through suffering, at which he can accept the fact that he is not God, he is able to establish a relationship of creative trust, i.e., "faith" in God. . . . This creative trust opens the door of one's heart to the grace or acceptance of God. It is when one feels accepted by God that one can "accept himself as being accepted," to use again

Tillich's phrase.[8]

"He loved us first!" (1 Jn 4:19). This is the message for alcoholics and their families; the message for all misusers of alcohol and their victims—and this is the church's message. This is the "should" of this book. It is the message my friends Dorene, Dave, Jean and Rudy heard! But there are millions more to hear it. So then, why are we, the church just "sitting there"?

Because you are reading this book, I assume that in some way you are asking the same question. My prayer is that God will give us the courage and hope that will involve us in this ministry to those suffering because of the abuse of alcohol. I also pray that this story of healing from Mark's Gospel will continue to inspire us as we learn concretely how we "can" do ministry with those in such great need.

Admittedly there are in our church community a fair number of concerned persons doing effective work with alcoholism and other alcohol problems, as well as with those suffering from other drug abuse. Yet in spite of the many churches who open their doors for AA, Al-Anon, Alateen and Adult Children of Alcoholics meetings, still in my experience, many people in the church community are not very knowledgeable about alcohol problems. Many that I have met in the church are embarrassed about dealing with alcohol-related problems. So we find today the pitiable fact that there are hundreds, more

---

[8] Howard J. Clinebell, *Understanding and Counseling the Alcoholic* (Nashville, TN, Abingdon, 1978) p. 158.

likely thousands, of churches in the United States where the subject is rarely mentioned, let alone where any sort of program is in force to deal with these ever-present problems.

So my deepest prayer is that churches around the country will listen to the call of God to this ministry so that the alcoholics, other alcohol abusers and the people whose lives they touch might be healed in body and spirit, freeing them from their bondage.

3

The Altar Call ❖

Even if you're on the right track, you'll get run over if you just sit there! —Will Rogers

This may be the most important chapter in this book—even though it is the shortest!

All the knowledge or conviction in the world will not do any good unless it produces action, just as all our teaching, sermons or sharing of need will do little good unless we ask for and get a commitment to action. To use religious jargon, we need to issue an "altar call" if we are looking for performance and change.

In some religious circles, this traditional evangelistic practice is downplayed, perhaps because of abuses. However, asking people to make a decision and linking this decision to action is basically a good spiritual and psychological ploy. Such altar calls need not be limited to mass rallies or to evangelistic efforts. Some of the most far-reaching decisions have been made where two or three are gathered, or even where one is "gathered" alone with God. In fact, aren't all decisions to serve God actually made individually—one to one with God?

God's call to the Apostle Paul while he was on his way to Damascus is one of the more powerful Person to person encounters recounted in the Scriptures (Ac 26:12-20). After being struck to the ground by a light more brilliant than the sun, Paul heard the Lord say to him, "Rise to your feet and stand upright. I have appeared to you for a purpose." Paul obeyed, got up and began his ministry which reverberates to this day.

By answering such altar calls we can follow in the footsteps of St. Paul and with dedicated effort reach many stumbling and lost people who need to hear the message of God's love, compassion, grace and healing. They in turn can rise to their feet to carry on this witness to others.

Our challenge is to hear this call to rise up. The time for sitting and taking our ease is gone. We must commit ourselves in thought and action to do something about the mission call before us. We in the church must meet the needs of those in the grip of alcoholism and other alcohol problems. A serious commitment to this ministry will strengthen as we proceed. I can guarantee from my own experience there will be joy unspeakable when we see lives saved and changed because we accepted Christ's call to speak words of truth to those who are seemingly hopeless because of the tragic effects of alcohol abuse.

PART II

THE CHURCH CAN ❖

4

Getting Started ❖

You can be the leader and take the first steps to get your church started in alcohol ministry. All it takes is one dedicated person to start a movement!

As I am writing this, the media has been retelling the story of Rear Admiral Grace Hopper who is retiring from the U.S. Navy at the age of 79. Years ago, seeing the need, she invented the widely used computer language known as COBOL. Her fame came from being a daring leader, always challenging the bureaucracy; a woman in a man's world and recently a senior citizen star in a field dominated by the very young. No wonder she is called "Amazing Grace!"

In the alcohol field, there is Candy Lightner—who considered herself an ordinary suburban mother in Sacramento, California, until her daughter was killed by a drunk driver. When she made up her mind to do something about drunk driving, she was laughed at both in the California Legislature and everywhere else. But she did it! Her persistence and hard work have brought about strict new laws against drunk driving across the country. Candy bonded together with other women and organized Mothers Against Drunk Driving (MADD) which spread throughout the U.S. and now into other countries, influencing legislation wherever it has appeared. She paid a price in time and energy and loss of naïveté, but what an accomplishment!

Taking a cue from Candy, all you need to do to start is to stand up and start! The first step on this exciting pilgrimage is to find two or three other like-minded persons to form a steering committee with you. Include your pastor in this group if at all possible. With this embryonic group, get together to talk and share experiences, brainstorm, suggest others who might enlist in the project and most of all—before, during and after—*pray*.

Pray that you will feel God's warmth, direction and strength every step of the way. Pray that you will have the courage to be the answer to your own prayers. Ask God to bind your group together in zeal and comradeship, and ask God to send healing to any of you who might be facing alcohol problems. Lastly, pray for those whom you do not yet know about, or may never know about, who will hear the good news of release from suffering because you dared to stand up and act. Then go to work.

Begin immediately to enlarge on the ideas that were generated in this first brainstorming session. Invite those on your "possibles" list to a get-together to ponder and add their ideas to yours. Begin assembling a library or portfolio of information you may have on hand about alcohol problems. Plan an in-depth study and begin thinking about possible projects. Do not despair if your group is not large. This is an uphill job for which not everyone will volunteer, but the view is magnificent when you get to the top! Commitment, willingness to risk, grow and endure are the essential qualities for the task.

I have found from my experience that it's important to decide early on something definite to "do" even as you are learning. Your task force or committee will thrive on action. It may be a simple project like surveying your community for sources of information, visiting treatment centers or listing relevant books which are in your public library; or it may be a more ambitious one involving an actual service.

When the group with which I was first involved decided almost immediately to set up a much needed half-way house for alcoholics, many people were willing to help. As there had been an earlier thwarted attempt which had involved much preliminary study, we were able to proceed on that information—successfully this time. And it became a hands-on learning project because we were motivated to continue studying the whole spectrum of alcohol problems as we progressed.

In my experience, study and action complement each other. Even though study and planning are essential, and making a survey and writing out a purpose are good things to do, I have also found that rewriting the purpose or re-listing goals and objectives over and over is a superbly effective way to avoid action and stifle the project to death. So try to begin implementing the program as soon as possible. Continue planning and evaluating realistically as you go along, but remember that when people are involved with action they will remain interested and you will achieve success. Even when problems arise, you will have moved in the direction of progress and be heading toward your overall goal.

If instead of a ministry within your congregation you envision a district-wide or an ecumenical organization, talk to the key persons charged with social concerns and to the executives or bishops. Enlist influential people to be on the initial steering committee and proceed with the same strategies listed above. If the project is ecumenical, get representatives from each church to serve on your study and planning group.

A final option could be to gather together persons in your community who are interested to begin the action. If possible, keep the study and projects under the aegis of the local church for purposes of support and developing interest and to keep it spiritually centered.

Some final points: you may feel the need for help as you proceed. Your local National Council on Alcoholism office or a community treatment program can find someone who can advise you. Inviting such experts to your group will get a relationship started. Your pastor, an executive from the local "Y" or similar group might be willing to help you develop an organization strategy.

Check to see what groups are represented on your task force. Are any alcoholics, their relatives or families included? Any persons involved with drunk driving? Any young people? What is the ratio of men to women? What professional, economic and social strata are included? Are the minorities in your church or area represented? Try to include representatives of as many groups as possible and draw from the community at large, if possible. You may get some good workers thus. As you build the membership of your task force, try to enlist one or two strong leaders from the constituency in which you propose to work. However, do not despair if you are unable to enlist those whom you approach. If they are uninterested or unavailable, work hard and faithfully and God will create new movers and shakers!

As you begin your search for knowledge and opportunities for alcohol ministry, you will be amazed at the amount of information available in printed form, seminars, audiovisuals, conversation and workshops. No doubt much of this is due to concern in the health and related fields about the dimension of alcohol problems in the country discovered as a result of new research and interest triggered by the passage of the Hughes Act in 1970 with its attendant publicity and provision of money.

As health professionals probed ever deeper in efforts to alleviate the consequences of alcoholism and other alcohol problems, they began to publish their findings and share their knowledge through public media. This book, too, is one more attempt to raise the public's interest but is intended especially to motivate those in the church to get involved in helping to solve this vast problem. To lay the groundwork for developing specific skills by a church wanting to minister to the needs brought on by the unwise use of alcohol in our modern society, a certain amount of study is almost mandatory.

What follows is an endeavor to assist in such a study.

To begin with, a basic knowledge of alcohol and its use and abuse is necessary. To assist in systematically acquiring such information, a comprehensive syllabus is included in Appendix I. Also, the three following chapters deal with related subjects which are often neglected: "What the Bible Says about Drinking," "The Spiritual Dimension" and "Alcohol Abuse vs. Alcoholism." These are issues which have been raised repeatedly in workshops which I have conducted and because they are often ignored, I feel they need clarification in order to understand much of what is said about the ministry of the church and alcohol problems.

The study of the Syllabus and the following chapters can be done individually, but it would be doubly fruitful if done together in the organizing task force. By using these materials as a springboard for discussion in relation to your own specific projects, it can become a hands-on experience. All can read the materials beforehand, or various ones in the group may take turns in studying a specific subject, then report to the group.

Beyond this, knowledgeable community persons can be invited to share their experience. Other beneficial activities are to attend workshops and training schools offered by local alcohol programs, universities, state and national organizations (see a list of these in the Appendix).

5

What the Bible Says About Drinking ❖

What does the Bible say about drinking—alcoholic beverages, that is? This is a frequent and legitimate question, but one which often brings confusing and contradictory answers which are sketchy—and blurred at best. In my own research into this topic, I set about to find authoritative information and interpretation of what the Bible says about the subject. I found little being said in the Bible commentaries which I consulted, but several Bible dictionaries provided good information.[9]

Further, to my surprise, in the more or less mainstream of religious publications, I discovered few articles

---

[9] These are listed in the Appendix - Resources (p. 203).

41

or books which dealt with what the Scriptures say about drinking. Occasionally I would stumble across a sentence or two interjected into writings dealing with general aspects of alcohol problems, but these were few and far between.

An obvious reason for such omissions is that the Bible does not give specific instructions on the use of alcoholic beverages which are adaptable to our life-style today. There is also disagreement about the interpretation of the meaning of the original words that refer to wine in particular scripture references. Difficult, also, is the possibility that an honest study might upset firmly held temperance / abstinence views or call into question the viability of one's current drinking habits. Finally, some biblical scholars dodge the issue, claiming it is not a major theme of scriptures.

Nevertheless, if the Scriptures are the "indispensable guide for the Christian faith and life,"[10] it seems that the serious Christian is hardly at liberty to ignore what they say about this subject, or any other.

It is my conviction that the Bible *does* make some clear and understandable statements about the use and misuse of alcoholic drinks. Thus Christians are called to make honest and forthright interpretations of the Scripture as well as to remain wary of conclusions reached through faulty theology, prejudices or manipulation. These latter two appear to be a particular temptation in

---

[10] "Brief Statement of Belief," *Book of Confessions, Presbyterian Church (U.S.A.)*, (New York: Office of the General Assembly, 1983) p. xiii.

regard to Scriptures which speak of the use of these beverages.[11]

To maintain honesty, while remembering that the Bible was written in another time and another land, we must remember that it remarkably and firmly communicates its message to us for today. As an exercise, we will consider representative passages of Scripture, accepting them for what they plainly say and then relate them, with honesty and candor, to other passages to help us interpret the message for us today.

❧ ❧ ❧

As I look out my windows here in California during the winter or early spring, I often see birds around the

[11] In the early days of the North American colonies, the Puritans and other settlers strove to practice temperance as they regularly imbibed their beer and wine. However, as more people of varying origins arrived, the drinking picture became confused and began to be characterized by bold and pernicious intemperance which in turn caused serious social problems. Observing these conditions, the great preachers of the 18th century, among them Increase Mather, Jonathan Edwards, and Timothy Dwight, spoke out forcefully against the excesses. In 1743, John Wesley left temperance behind, and proclaimed abstinence as the only acceptable alternative. From 1800 on, Lyman Beecher became the great preacher of abstinence. Methodist pastors, followed by Baptists, and then Presbyterian ministers, were all adjured by their superiors to preach abstinence. To support their position, these churches and others emphasized the Scriptures which referred to the negative effects of alcohol and often skewed others to suit their purposes—all of which might be considered honorable in the face of the over-riding problem of drunkenness then existing—but nevertheless not fully honest, hermeneutically speaking.

pyracantha or other bushes greedily devouring berries which are obviously past their prime. These busy birds return again and again, madly gobbling these berries despite their spoiled condition. Some folks say they have seen these eager birds staggering after a good meal of overripe berries!

Possibly such a simple observation caused our long ago ancestors to experience the tastiness and salutary effect of grapes which had hung on the vine too long. When they began to process those grapes in an orderly fashion—however primitively—to produce wine, they started an industry that has been flourishing ever since. Beer also was discovered early. Manufactured readily from starchy plants, it was a favorite in Egypt. We have murals chiseled in stone slabs and decorating household vessels from ancient times which are historical records attesting that wine was common in everyday life and enjoyed frequently, but was likewise a problem on occasion. Our earliest recorded history notes the centrality of the use of wines or beer which were used "in all significant personal and social occasions; in religious ritual; in all rites of passage from birth to initiation to marriage to funeral; in all public happenings; in compacts, feasts, conclaves, crownings, war-making and peace-making; in hospitality, magic and medicine."[12]

This everyday use of alcoholic beverages was part of

---

[12] Mark Keller, "A Historical Overview of Alcohol and Alcoholism," (Address to the Alcohol and Cancer Workshop, October 23, 1978, Bethesda, MD; available from Rutgers School of Alcohol Studies, p. 2822)

all the early civilizations of the Middle East. Grapes are mentioned growing in Mesopotamia in 3,000 B.C. and wild grapes were reported in Asia Minor in 1,500 B.C. Noah, after coming out of the ark, was called the first tiller of the soil as he planted a vineyard about 2,800 B.C. (Gn 9:20).

The Greeks and the Romans commonly made and drank wine. The Greeks believed that the god Dionysus discovered wine and that, in fact, it was his blood and that "with the wine, god entered into you so that for a time you partook of the godhead."[13]

Sometime during the first or second century B.C. it became customary to dilute wine with water. Proportions varied from two or three parts water to one of wine, but often consisted of more water—up to 20 parts water to one of wine on one recorded occasion. One-to-one was considered by some ancients as "strong wine" whereas drinking it straight was a barbarian custom.[14] From larger bowls into which it was first poured, wine was poured into smaller bowls, analogous to current-day cups, for individual consumption. These vessels were made of gold and silver in palaces and temples but more commonly of wood, pottery or stone in ordinary households.

Among both Greeks and Romans women were at first forbidden to drink intoxicating beverages, but later they

---

[13] Charles Saltman, *Wine in the Ancient World,* (London: Rutledge, Kegan, Paul, Ltd., 1957) p. 21.

[14] Robert H. Stein, "Wine-Drinking in New Testament Times," *Christianity Today* (June 20, 1975) p. 9 and Gaalyahu Cornfeld, ed., *Pictorial Biblical Encyclopedia* (New York: Macmillan Co., 1964) p. 334.

were allowed to do so on certain occasions. Permitted or no, in Greece some women drank wine while their men were away at war! Every other year, the legitimate pilgrimage to Delphi by the Thyads—the mystic god-possessed women of Athens—was a wild occasion where they drank their fill of wine. In Rome the Bacchanalian rites (Bacchus was the Roman name for Dionysus) among women were relatively harmless until men were admitted (!) when they became orgies which were so debauched they were finally banned in 176 B.C. Unfortunately, through such activities in both the Greek and Roman cultures, these women established reputations which haunt women in Western culture to this day.

It was in this Mediterranean, Middle East milieu, that the people of the Bible lived. The climate and land's topography dictated their agricultural pursuits and life-style and the cultivation of grapes was a natural part of ordinary farming endeavors. They did not live isolated from each other as they migrated, travelled or traded throughout their world using the anciently developed transportation system to exchange cuttings and hints about cultivating the vines and making wine.

I can clearly envision all this from my home here in the San Joaquin Valley of California with its climate similar to that of the Middle East which makes this one of the great grape-growing regions of the world. Markets all over the U.S. and throughout the world sell our table-grapes, raisins and the wine from our world-famous wineries. The original cuttings, along with the wine- and raisin-making skills, were brought here by immigrants from the Mediterranean countries.

Often it is said that Middle Easterners traditionally drank wine because their water was impure and scarce. This is a disputed point, for potable water was usually available in streams or cisterns and taken for granted as is indicated in many Biblical accounts. People drank water gladly in such a climate (*Strong's Concordance* lists over two pages of references to water in the Scriptures.) Although there may have been times of scarcity in the dry season, water seems to have been present for daily use, and like many other simple and precious everyday substances, water was used symbolically in both the Old and New Testaments and other holy writings.

One last comment: Muslims who are forbidden to drink alcohol have of necessity drunk water (often as coffee) and survived quite well for centuries in the same region.

Wine and Drinking in the Old Testament

Wine is mentioned for better or worse in the Old Testament over 2,000 times. Related words incorporating the word "wine," e.g., winebibber, winepress, winefat, occur 18 times. Words indicating strong drink, drinking, eating and drinking—probably of wine of some sort—and drunk and drunkard occur close to 100 times. In another category, drink offerings of wine, the libation which was part of the sacrificial ceremonies, occur well over 30 times.[15]

---

[15] James Strong, *The New Strong's Exhaustive Concordance of the*

The first specific mention of wine in the Bible is in the story of Noah who, in an incident less than noble, drank wine which no doubt was made from grapes from his new, post-Flood vineyard, got drunk and disgraced himself by passing out in his tent where he was discovered naked by his sons (Gn 9:20-25). The word used here is *yayin* which is the word most used for wine throughout the Old Testament, occurring in 32 books. It occurs in all types and styles of writings in the Old Testament—law, history, poetry and prophecy—so it would appear to be the most common word for wine in the Hebrew vocabulary and was passed on from generation to generation.

Yayin definitely refers to fermented wine. This is easily deduced from the many untoward incidents described when too much *yayin* was imbibed, as in Noah's case, and from considering the system and conditions under which wine was made. The latter involved picking the grapes when they were at their best for wine, carrying them to a winepress usually made of stone where they were trampled—often with much singing and shouting—to press out the juice which then dripped into a vat below.[16]

Fermentation begins immediately as the grapes are picked because of the "must" on them. This splashy, hard, but joyous, work took place in late August or early September—hot months in that clime—so fermentation could hardly be arrested at this point.

Bible (Nashville, TN: Thomas Nelson, 1984).
[16] The *Pictorial Biblical Encyclopedia,* pp. 19-20, shows pictures of wine presses from the Post-Exilic Period which are still in existence.

The next stage involved pouring the fermenting juice into wineskins or large pottery jars for further fermentation. The wineskins were made from new, whole goatskins with the openings tied securely shut, except for one which functioned as a vent for the escaping carbon dioxide gas formed by the fermentation process. John Spahr describes this step graphically:

> Ancient people seemed always to choose descriptive and picturesque words to indicate the things of life going on in their world. Lacking precise information about gases and just what was going on in the fermentation process, they simply reported what they saw, communicating their intrigue with the bubbling up of the carbon dioxide. Observing the heat that was being given off and all that mysterious bubbling, they thought they were seeing boiling. Their word *chamar* (kaw-mar) which literally means "to boil up" or "to foam", they took as their word for fermenting. What they saw was somewhat like the boiling up of a storm across the Sea of Galilee, or even what they imagined was going on inside an upset stomach—boiling, bubbling, foaming, fermenting.[17]

When the bubbling and foaming had pretty much subsided, the redolent liquid, if in wineskins, was transferred to jars or bottles where it remained for a period of weeks or months in order to develop flavor and bouquet. The fermentation continued slowly until all the sugar

---

[17] John Howard Spahr, *Sober Life* (Pittsburgh, PA: Dorrance and Co.) pp. 7-8.

was converted to alcohol which usually was ten to twelve percent of the total volume.

This fully aged beverage was called *yayin*—almost in a generic sense—much as we use our word "wine" today. There were variations of this basic *yayin* and although they are identified by different Hebrew words, they are translated into English, more often than not, simply as wine. Following is a list of such variations with meanings, pronunciations and relative intoxication levels.[18]

tirosh (tee-roshe') — refers to the "must" or freshly squeezed grape juice; sometimes called new-wine; light in alcohol content (only example of this really fresh juice being served is in Gn 40:11).

aciye (aw-sees') — similar to *tirosh* (Is 49:26).

chemer (keh'-mer) — pure red wine; the grapes ordinarily planted were red and juice was called the blood of the grape (Is 27:2 [KJV]).

chamar (kham-mar')—fermentation, definitely intoxicating (Ezr 6:9; Dn 5:1, 2, 4; 5:23).

shekar (shay-kawr') — intoxicating, intensely alcoholic liquor; paired with wine in the expression "wine and strong-drink." May also have been made from other fruits, (Pr 20:1; Is 28:7).

mamcak (mam-sawk')—wine mixed with water and spices; used for drink offering at sacrifices (Pr 23:30).

chamets (kaw-mates') — sour in taste; or

chomets (kho-mets') — vinegar or poor quality wine (Rt

---

[18] Compiled from *Strong's Concordance and Hebrew Lexicon.* The Bible references given here are only samples of usage. In most cases there are many more.

2:14).

enab (ay-nawb´) — the ripe grape or the red wine made from them (Gn 40:10; 49:11; Nb 13:23).

shemer (sheh´—mer) — lees or sediment which was strained from aged wine as it was poured through a cloth into large bowls in preparation for serving. It was often put into wine which was still aging in order to improve its flavor, color and strength. This could well have been the "strong drink" frequently spoken of (Is 25:6).

There were also significant words related to the use of wine which are translated as 1) *drink, drank* or *drinking;* or 2) *drunk* or *drunken.*

In determining the meaning of those in the first group, it is important to consider the context, for other liquids were commonly imbibed, such as milk or water, and were mentioned in tandem with ordinary daily eating. However, one Hebrew word used repeatedly to indicate that wine was the particular beverage referred to when discussing "eating and drinking" was *shathah* (shaw-thaw´). Its root means to imbibe, but evidently it grew to indicate a relationship to the word banquet, then to the word drink and finally to drunk(en). Over-imbibing is not always implied in the Biblical accounts of eating and drinking wine, but there are many events where it definitely is mentioned and there are other stories when one wonders if it ought not to have been! (Gn 24:54; Rt 3:3; I K 4:20; I Ch 12:39; Ec 2:24 and 5:18).

In an entirely different category was the use of the Hebrew word *necek* (nay-sek´) which meant the "drink offering" or libation presented at the time of offering the sacrifices on the altars in the tabernacle or in the temple. A libation, according to the dictionary,[19] consisted of "pouring a liquid (as wine) either on the ground or on a victim in a sacrifice to the deity" (Ex 29:40).

The second group of drink-related words which are translated for us as *drunk* and *drunken* indicate without doubt the conditions they describe, even when they were not necessarily caused by too much wine (cf 1 S 1:14,15). There are not many specific Hebrew words which mean drunkenness, but in this list you will notice some similarity with the words meaning wine:

> *shakar* (shaw-kar') — to become tipsy, make drunk, be filled with drink (2 S 11:13—actual; Is 63:6—symbolic).
> *shikkowr* (shik-kore') — intoxicated, as a state or habit (Is 24:20).
> *shikkarown* (shik-kaw-rone') — intoxication, drunkenness (Gn 9:21—actual; Jr 13:13—symbolic).
> *cobe* (so-beh') — drink, drunken; includes winebibber—very emphatic (Dt 21:20; Pr 23:21).
> *shethiy* (sheth-ee') — intoxication, drunkenness.

It appears that whenever these words are used they are meant to give a strong message!

Finally, wine grapes are produced on vines which in those days were grown in vineyards or informally on or around the outside of the house. There are about 60 references to vines *(gephen* [gheh'-fen]) in the Old Testa-

---

[19] *Third New International Dictionary* (Springfield, MA: Merriam-Webster, Inc. 1981)

ment and about 90 to vineyards *(kerem* [keh'-rem]). A farmer's vineyard was a treasured possession and was faithfully cared for. This great value, no doubt, is why vines and vineyards are used so often to illustrate blessings or judgments throughout the Scriptures, particularly in Old Testament prophetic messages. (See for *gephen* — Dt 8:8; Jr 5:17; *kerem* — Ps 107:37—blessing; Is 5:1-7—judgment; Gn 22:5—value.)

❧ ❧ ❧

The many references in the Old Testament which use the words for wine, strong drink, drinking and drunken describe the use of alcoholic beverages in those times. Wine—its production and consumption—was a part of the everyday life of both the chosen people of God and their neighboring nations. In homes that could afford it, wine was a common part of the hearty meal of the day and was almost always included in the meals set before visitors and travelers in accordance with the standards of hospitality of that day (Jg 19:4-8, 22). The travelers themselves probably had a supply in their provisions for the journey (Jg 19:19).

Wine was also given as a gift to important persons or on special occasions (I S 16:19-20; 2 S 16:1, 2) and it was a significant part in the celebration of all momentous events[20] (1 Ch 12:40; 29:21, 22). Wine was used medicinally as an antiseptic, anesthetic and to soothe internal

---

[20] See quote from Keller, p. 44, this work.

disturbances (2 S 16:2; cf. 1 Tm 5:23; Mt 27:34, 48; Mk 15:23, 36). It was such an accepted part of life that rations of it were regularly issued to one's workers (2 Ch 2:10, 15; Ezr 7:22) and to the soldiers in the army (I K 20:12ff).[21]

By and large, the uses of wine in Old Testament days do not sound strange to us for they are similar to how wine is used today in most cultures. The religious use of wine in the Old Testament was major. Wine is routinely mentioned in the tripartite list of "grain, wine and oil" which made up the offerings brought to the Temple, particularly for the Feast of the Firstfruits at the time of the spring equinox and for the Feast of the Ingathering or Harvest at the time of the fall equinox (Ex 23:16). The wine, having been recently produced, was especially important at the latter feast. A tithe was taken from these gifts and given to the priests, the Levites, for their living (Dt 18:4) and they in turn gave a tithe to the high priest, a linear descendant of Aaron.

Eating and drinking played a prominent part in the observance of all the feasts which were occasions for praise, rejoicing and having a good time. However, one can speculate that after several days—seven in the case of the Feast of Tents (Ne 8:14-18)—of such merriment there were problems brought on by over-imbibing.

Grain, oil and wine are mentioned over and over at the time of making the ritual sacrifices of expiation as

---

[21] Rum and whiskey were distributed to U.S. soldiers in the early days. See Mark Edward Lender and James Kirby Martin, *Drinking in America* (New York: The Free Press, 1982) pp. 31 & 32.

the indispensable accompaniments to the sacrifices (Ex 29:40-42; Lv 23:13-14). They are often called grain offerings and drink offerings.

Wine as a libation was poured either on the animal victim, on the four corners of the altar or on the ground. Wine, usually being red, was sometimes called the blood of the grape (Gn 49:11; Dt 32:14). Since the blood of the animal was also poured or sprinkled on the altar in expiatory symbolism, it is not difficult to grasp the significance of the wine as we read of Jesus giving the cup to his disciples at the last supper (Mt 26:28, 29; I Co 11:25, 26).

Another view of wine in the Old Testament was that it symbolized a grace from God. A plenteous supply was looked upon as a sign of the Covenant, a specific blessing in return for honoring God by obedience (Gn 27:28; Dt 7:13; 11:14; Pr 3:9, 10). It was seen as a part of God's magnificent providence in sustaining and providing pleasure in life (Ps 104:14, 15). We read that during the peaceful and prosperous reign of Solomon "the people of Judah and Israel were countless as the sands of the sea; they ate and they drank and enjoyed life!" (1 K 4:20, 25).

Although he was busy with many projects, including building the temple, promoting liaisons with his neighboring kings—many through marriage—Solomon found time to write prolifically. He is generally thought to be the author of Proverbs, Ecclesiastes and Song of Songs in which he refers often to wine as a symbol of God's favor and frequently uses it in similes to describe the beauty and joys of other blessings (Ec 9:7; 10:19; Sg 1:2, 4; 4:10; 5:1; Pr 3:9, 10). However we should note that Song of

Songs (4:10) does claim that love is better than wine!

Perhaps the clearest indication that wine was keenly appreciated by the Old Testament people as a blessing from God is found in the many references to its disappearance as a result of God's judgment on recalcitrant Israel for disobedience and its reappearance—with great joy—when they repented and once again sought to obey God's commandments. This seesaw of disobedience / judgment followed by repentance / blessing is described again and again beginning in Deuteronomy—when the 40 year sojourners in the wilderness were forbidden to drink wine—continuing on through the graphic descriptions of their frequent episodes—past, present and future—of straying and returning. Such accounts are very prominent in the prophets (Is 1:22; 5:1-10; 36:17; 62:8; 65:8; Jr 31:12; Ho 2:8, 12; 7:14; 9:2, 4; 14:7; Jl 1:10; 2:19, 24; 3:18; Am 5:11; 9:13, 14; Mi 6:15; Zp 1:13; Zc 10:7).

The marvelous poetry of Isaiah and Jeremiah records similar judgments befalling the heathen who were often admired by Israel and Judah (Babylon—Jr 51:7, 8, 36-39, 57; false religions—Jr 8:13; Moab—Jr 48:33; Is 16:10; general—22:13).

Although many of the incidents with which the prophets deal are historical, their message reaches far beyond them to the future—the final restoration, the new Jerusalem, the Day of the Lord. Amos says that the mountains will run with fresh wine (9:13-14); Joel says the vats will overflow with oil and wine (2:24); and Isaiah says there will be a feast of wine (25:6) and foreigners will not make off with the wine you have labored to make (62:8)!

The idea of wine being a grace from God is difficult to accept by many conscientious persons who ask: "How can anything which causes so much trouble be a grace, a special gift from God?" John Spahr answers that the people of the Bible in their simplicity accepted "wine as a logical symbol of the elevated mood of joy and celebration in the worship of God," and that they could do this because they had "not lived through the days of the abstinence crusades nor in the swirl of their wake. There was a freedom to celebrate God and to celebrate [God] with wine."[22]

Finally, in answer to the shock the teetotaler feels upon realizing the ancients' ready acceptance of wine as a grace from God, we need to remember that there are many joys in life for which we praise God when they are experienced in the proper milieu which can become hell on earth when abused—like the beautiful and licit sexual love between a man and a woman; the trusting, mutual love of child and parent; and the bosom / kindred-spirit friendship between two people.

Indeed, there is another aspect to the issue of wine in the Old Testament. Despite its being considered a grace of God, it was routinely misused causing much trouble and sorrow. Besides Noah's notable episode (Gn 9:21-24), we find Jacob stealing his brother Esau's birthright after weakening his father with wine (Gn 27:25); and Lot's daughters using a similar ploy to establish two more bloodlines who eventually became the enemies of Israel

---

[22] Spahr, p. 17.

(Gn 19:31-38).

Manipulation of others, while they were under the influence, appeared to be a favorite pastime of those in power. Wine flowed freely in the Persian court of King Ahasuerus. His first queen, Vashti, was banished because she would not submit to his drunken requests. Her more famous successor, Esther, however, used her husband's drunkenness to her own advantage in one of the most enthralling stories of intrigue ever written (Est 1:7-22; 5:1-14; 7:1-10). David, the "man after God's own heart," used wine as a prominent element in his adulterous affair with Bathsheba and the subsequent plot to kill her husband, Uriah, whom David arranged to be "made drunk" under the guise of friendship. Although David repented sorrowfully for his sins and was mercifully forgiven by God, the horrendous events occurring subsequently within his family were sent in judgment by God, haunting David for the rest of his life (2 S 11:11-15; 12:10-14).

As we read story after story of the early days of Israel where excessive eating and drinking were indicated specifically or at least implied, can we not legitimately wonder how much of the barbarous and wild behavior of the Old Testament folk—both Israelite and others—was brought on by too much wine or strong drink? Or did they deaden their sensitivities with alcohol, thus psyching themselves to perform the ferocious acts they had in mind?

Another indication that drunkenness was prevalent is implied in the story of unhappy Hannah who eventually became the mother of the prophet, Samuel. While silently pleading with God in the Temple that she be given offspring, she was reprimanded by the priest Eli who saw her lips moving but heard no sound. "Enough of this drunken behavior," he said. "Go away until the wine has worn off" (1 S 1:14, 15).

In the Psalms, Proverbs, Isaiah, Jeremiah and Hosea we find passages filled with colorful and pejorative language to describe the drinker: staggering, reeling, quarrelsome, bloodshot eyes, anxiety, hallucinations, confusion of thought and speech, insensitivity to physical injury, preoccupation with drinking, being inflamed (flushing), unjust in dealings, warped in judgment, vomiting, clamoring, stupor, hiccuping, filthy, falling, madness—to name a few! (Ps 60:3; 107:27; Pr 23:33, 35; 26:9; Is 5:11, 22; 19:14; 28:7, 8; 51:20; Jr 25:27; 51:7; Ho 4:11).

Proverbs gives us some straightforward warnings: A person who loves wine or keeps company with drunkards will never grow rich and the wine business itself is fraught with trouble, even violence (Pr 4:17; 21:17; 23:20, 21). Both Isaiah and Proverbs describe what we now call alcoholism (Is 5:11, 12; Pr 23:29-35) and amazingly, the fetal alcohol syndrome was seemingly recognized as far back as the time of the Judges! (Jg 13:4, 5, 11).[23]

Although we discover no laws per se forbidding the drinking of wine or other alcoholic beverages,[24] the inci-

---

[23] The Greeks also recorded having observed the effect of drinking on the fetus. See Marian Sandmaier, *The Invisible Alcoholics* (New York: McGraw-Hill, 1980) p. 26.

[24] For three special groups, wine was forbidden: 1) the Rechabites,

dents, comments and admonitions involving drunkenness definitely show us that such behavior was absolutely unacceptable.

According to the Old Testament, temperate sobriety was to be maintained through self-control. Feasting was to be carried on within the limits of self-control. Isaiah pronounced shame on topers who perverted justice (5:22). Proverbs 23, in describing alcoholism, gives several hints for avoiding trouble: don't linger late over wine; don't get caught up in experimenting with new spiced liquor; don't gulp it; don't keep company with drunkards. Later Proverbs quotes King Lemuel's mother who has pithy advice for kings and princes including the admonition that they should not crave strong drink lest they forget the laws and pervert the rights of the afflicted (31:4).[25]

Some idea of the depth of feeling about drunkenness can be learned from the "tough-love" provision set down in Deuteronomy (21:18-21) for dealing with unruly sons.

---

a nomadic people, not Israelites but dwelling among them, who kept the vow of abstinence which their ancestor Jonadab had made (Jr 35:1-17); 2) the Nazarites, who personally took vows for a specific period or for life to let their hair grow, abstain from intoxicating drink and keep away from dead bodies (Samson was probably the most notable Nazarite in the Old Testament [Nb 6:1-8] while John the Baptist was the foremost New Testament example [Lk 7:33]); and 3) the Priests were forbidden to drink wine or strong drink when they went into the Tabernacle and later the Temple, in order that they would have their wits about them during the important rites of sacrifice (Lv 10:9-11).

[25] Some puzzling advice follows in vv. 6 & 7—"give strong drink to the desperate and wine to the embittered" so they will forget their poverty. Such advice runs against our grain, but such was actually done in our country on holidays for the American slaves and indentured servants according to Lender and Martin (pp. 27, 28).

A despairing mother and father were to bring their recalcitrant offspring to the elders at the gate (where the elders, or judges, sat regularly to settle disputes among the people) and there report that "this son is disobedient, out of control . . . a wastrel and a drunkard." The son then was to be stoned to death by all the men of the town—which is a bit severe according to our sensibilities and legal standards.

Wine and Drinking in the New Testament

In turning to look at what the New Testament and Jesus had to say about alcoholic beverages, we should note that this second part of our Bible is not only much shorter in length than the Old Testament, but it covers a much briefer time period—100 years over against 2,000 years. The New Testament is also not as remote historically from our culture and thus feels more familiar to us. However, there are still wide cultural differences that preclude our being able to deduce, understand or accept what it says about the issues revolving around alcohol consumption. We thus must turn to available scholarship to help us interpret honestly what we find here.

Hellenistic Greek was the vernacular of the far-flung Roman Empire and is the language in which the New Testament books were written. This providentially permitted their circulation throughout the empire. Hellenistic Greek has only two words used specifically for wine:

oinos (oy´-nos) meaning simply wine. Probably used to

mean the same as *yayin, chemer* and *tiyrosh* in the Old Testament, it occurs 23 times.

gleukos (glyoo'-kos) refers to new wine, but also was used of sweet, saccharine wine which made it more inebriating and occurs only once (Ac 2:13).

In addition there are two words which mean wine when considered in context:

gennema (ghen'-nay-mah) meaning fruit of the vine, is used three times (Lk 22:18; Mt 26:28; Mk 14:25).

sikera (sik'-er-ah) indicated intensely fermented liquor, i.e., "strong drink" and is used once (Lk 1:15).

There are several words, used once or twice, to indicate drunken or drunkenness:

paroinas (par'-oy-nas) meaning given to wine (I Tm 3:3; Tt 1:7).

oinophulgia (oy-nof-loog-ee') — excess of wine (I P 4:3).

oinapotes (oy-nap-ot'-ace) — tippler, winebibber (Mt 11:9; Lk 7:34).

methuo (meth-oo'-o) — make or be drunk (Mt 24:49; Ac 2:15).

methusko (meth-oos'-ko) — to intoxicate, be drunk (Lk 12:45).

methe (meth'-ay) — drunkenness (Lk 21:34; Rm 13:13; Ga 5:21).

Related words which probably include drunkenness are:

asotia (as-o-tee'-ah) meaning profligacy and excess (Lk 15:13; Ep 5:13).
kraipale (kra-hee-pal'-ay) also meaning drunkenness (Lk 2:34).

John Spahr says the former can also be translated "debauchery" while the latter means "dissipation . . . hangover".[26]

Two words are used to indicate winepress:

lenos (lay-nos') — (Mt 21:33; Rv 14:19; 19:15).
hupolenion (hoop-ol-oy'-nee-on) which refers to the receptacle or lower wine vat placed under the press to catch the juice (Mk 12:1).

Two words related to vineyard and vine are used repeatedly in the New Testament:

ampelon (am-pel-ohn') — vineyard.
ampelos (am'-pel-os) — vine.

Another word, *pino* (pee'no), by extrapolation can be interpreted to mean to drink wine when it is used in certain connotations, e.g. , "eating and drinking." It is used nine times (Lk 5:33; 12:19, 45; 22:18; Rm 14:21; Mt 24:49; 1 Co 11:22-29).

In the opposite vein to drunkenness are two words:

nepho (nay'-fo) meaning to be sober or watch is used three

---

[26] Spahr, pp. 46, 48.

times in important contexts (1 Th 5:6 & 8; 1 P 1:13; 5:8).

sophroneo (so-fron-eh'-o) or *sophron* (so'-frone) is used several times to indicate soberness in the sense of being temperate or in one's right mind (2 Co 5:13; Tt 2:6; 1 P 4:7; 1 Tm 3:2; Tt 1:8).

❧ ❧ ❧

Of course the Jews of New Testament times lived according to Old Testament customs which had developed over centuries and become de rigueur by the time of Christ. As their ancestors had, they regarded the imbibing of wine as part of everyday life—deploring but accepting as a matter of course the problems that went with it. In their daily life and worship they were influenced by the practices of their neighbors and by those under whose subjugation they lived for extended periods of time.

In this specific context, what is said in the Gospels about alcohol and what did Jesus say and do?

Luke's gospel refers to wine—negatively—telling us of the miraculous birth of John the Baptist who "will be great in the eyes of the Lord. He shall never touch wine or strong drink" (1:15). John became a Nazarite, making and keeping a lifelong vow never to touch either substance. His mission during his ascetic life was to give witness to Jesus as the Messiah and the account of his extraordinary baptism of Jesus is well-known (Jn 1:6-18; Lk 3:15:22).

Three days after his baptism by John, Jesus went to a wedding in Cana with his mother and his disciples. As still the case in Middle Eastern and Asian countries, wedding celebrations were festive affairs, some lasting several days with much eating, drinking, dancing, games and contests. It took a lot of food and drink—including wine, of course—to care for all the guests. To run out of either, as they did at this wedding, was a disgrace.

What to do! After chiding his worried mother, Jesus turned the water in six huge stone jars into wine of better quality than that which had already been served (Jn 2:1-11).

This was Christ's first recorded miracle in the New Testament. The wonder of it we can readily appreciate, but the incident has been much maligned because it means, if accepted at face value, not only that Jesus probably drank wine with the other guests, but worse yet, he made it!

The Greek word used is plainly *oinos* meaning fermented wine. Knowing the customs of the day, there is no reason to doubt it was just that. We cannot in honesty twist it to mean, as some would like, that the wedding guests were drinking plain grape juice. T. Furman Hewitt says in regard to this incident that "no negative connotation to wine drinking is implied in the story and it may even reflect the Old Testament view that wine is the creation of God."[27]

John the Baptist's attitude toward drinking wine and Jesus' evident practice were brought together many

---

[27] T. Furman Hewitt, *A Biblical Perspective on the Use and Abuse of Alcohol and Other Drugs* (Raleigh, NC: North Carolina Department of Human Resources, 1980) p. 15.

months later as Jesus was speaking in praise of his cousin. Listening, the ever-present Pharisees and lawyers found basis for a whining complaint: John who didn't eat certain ordinary things and abstained from drinking wine was surely possessed of a devil; no better was this Jesus who was seen to eat and drink—him they called a glutton and a winebibber *(oinapotes)*—a friend of tax gathers and sinners (Mt 11:18, 19; Lk 7:33, 34; cf. Lk 5:30).

There is no indication in Scriptures that these charges of gluttony or drunkenness, like many others from this group of critics, are true. Clearly it was not the real issue, but rather an opportunity to discredit Jesus— which they continually sought to do throughout his ministry. It does imply, however, that Jesus probably drank wine—as well as water, milk, fruit juice or whatever was offered at the tables of his hosts.

A final indication of Christ's personal use of wine comes from the accounts of the Last Supper where Jesus says, "Never again shall I drink *(pino)* from the fruit of the vine *(gennema)* until that day when I drink it new with you in the kingdom of my Father." The implication is plainly that Jesus and his disciples were accustomed under ordinary circumstances to drinking wine, the fruit of the vine, at the Passover supper. We now know this was no ordinary meal, yet there is no reason to believe that anything but the usual wine was served (Mt 26:26-29; Mk 14:22-25; Lk 22:17-19).

Although accounts involving Christ's use of wine are limited, he frequently used illustrations involving vines, vineyards, wine and winepresses in his teaching. Obviously he knew his hearers understood such illustrations because of the prominence in their lives of viticulture.

One of the more beautiful passages in Scriptures is found in John 15:1-10 where Christ says, "I am the vine and you are the branches," as he describes the fruitful Christian life in familiar metaphors.

Christ also placed several parables about the Kingdom of God in vineyards referring to commonly known facts about vineyard husbandry: The laborers in the vineyard who were hired at different times of the day but were paid the same, to the consternation of those who were hired first (Mt 20:1-6); and the wicked tenants who refused to pay the owner's share from the produce and in their rebellion killed both the owner's servants and heir (Mt 21:33-43; Mk 12:1-9; Lk 20:9-16).

Other stories which Jesus told indicate his knowledge about wine, e.g., the Good Samaritan who used wine to clean the wounds of the mugged wayfarer (Lk 10:34); the metaphor of not putting new wine into old wineskins (Mt 2:22; 10:17; Lk 5:37, 38); and the plainly understood declaration that "The old wine is good!" (Lk 5:39).

To illustrate trustworthiness while waiting for the Son of Man to come, he talks about the inadvisability of drinking (*pino*) with drunken (*methuo*) friends in two vivid parables (Mt 24:49; Lk 12:42-46). Eating, drinking and making merry are also included in the parable about the foolishness of the greedy grower (Lk 12:17-21). Although the points of these parables are not primarily the drinking mentioned, they do illustrate how too much alcohol dulls the senses and facilitates bad behavior—a fact that might have been overlooked in that day and frequently is today! Apparently Jesus understood the connection.

In only one Scripture passage extant do we find Jesus specifically expressing disapproval of drunkenness:

Be on guard so that your hearts are not weighed down with dissipation and drunkenness and the worries of this life, and that day catch you unexpectedly, like a trap. For it will come upon all who live on the face of the whole earth (Lk 21:34, 35 [NRSV]).

These verses conclude a Passion Week discourse in the Temple about the troublous end times which will culminate in the coming of the Son of Man in a cloud. The word dissipation (*kraipale*), as stated earlier, refers to a headache which one experiences the morning after a drinking spree—a hangover. The drunkenness mentioned is severe drunkenness (*methe*). Jesus here could well be speaking about the blackout type of drunkenness which he says might cause you to miss the greatest event of all—his second coming.

Although it might be argued that Jesus is permitting "a little drunkenness," we know that with only a "couple of drinks" one's judgment is already being dulled, hence the admonition to "be on guard." A little drunkenness can too easily and quickly turn into a big drunk.

The riveting incident involving Jesus and alcoholic drink occurred at the Crucifixion when Jesus refused the proffered wine before they nailed him to the cross. Mark says it was mixed with myrrh, a painkilling drug. Of this horrifying spectacle at the cross, John Spahr says: "Our Lord was being offered a painkiller of which he had some need, but no need."[28] This was "saying no" in the ultimate (Mt 27:34; Mk 15:23 [RSV]).

Toward the end of the ordeal, a compassionate bystander soaked a sponge in cheap wine or vinegar and held it to Jesus' feverish, parched lips. After receiving a few moist drops, "He bowed his head and gave up his spirit" (Mt 24:48; Mk 15:36; Jn 19:29).

ૐ ૐ ૐ

Leaving the gospels we come to the book of Acts which starts with the extraordinary event of Pentecost—the birthday of the church—when spirits and the Spirit figure prominently. We know the story well: expatriate Jews, immigrants from many other countries and other foreign visitors listened as simple Galileans (actually Jesus' disciples) told them—miraculously in their native languages—the wonderful things that God had done in their midst.

Amazement and perplexity concerning this remarkable feat increased. Some accused these uneducated, excited speakers saying, "They have been drinking!" (gleukos). They appeared to be intoxicated! Peter, the feisty one, could not let such an accusation pass, so standing up and shouting, he began his power-filled sermon by saying:

Fellow Jews and all you who live in Jerusalem, mark

---

[28] Spahr, p. 49.

> *this and give me a hearing. These men are not drunk (methuo) as you imagine, for it is only nine in the morning. No, this is what the prophet spoke of . . . I will pour out upon everyone a portion of my spirit (2:14-17).*

That spirit was *pneuma* in the Greek or *spiritus* in Latin. In English the name Holy Spirit derives from the latter as does the word spirits meaning alcohol. This juxtaposition of derivatives might be understood from the timeless effort to seek out answers to the probing questions of human existence. Some have thought they could find answers and peace of mind in the euphoria of alcohol. So perhaps it was not so odd that these disciples of Christ who were newly filled and bubbling over with the Holy Spirit were judged to be drunk.

The 21 epistles that follow Acts deal with the ongoing life of the church as it was then—and as it is now—with guidelines for all Christians for study, inspiration and rules to live by. Surprisingly, only Paul and Peter have anything to say about using intoxicating beverages.

As in the Gospel period, the use of wine continued to be a fact of life among the Jews and all those who lived in the Diaspora in Asia Minor, Greece and Rome. Although it evidently never occurred to Paul or Peter to advocate total abstinence, there are several emphatic instructions about avoiding drunkenness. This emphasis would indicate that over-imbibing must have been common throughout the Græco-Roman world and was consequently a worrisome problem to be dealt with in the early churches.

The great missioner Paul who planted many churches among the Gentiles during his three missionary journeys was always eager to maintain lines of communication with the converts he had left behind. In his letters which he would send along with helpers who could intern in the various areas of the burgeoning church he would often write instructions for the new churches' edification. Thankfully, these letters continue to edify the church to this day.

We do not know if Paul, as Saul, had been in the crowd on the day of Pentecost, but he had some strong things to say to the Galatians and Ephesians about drunkenness vis-à-vis the Holy Spirit. He admonished them to seek to be filled with the Spirit who would guide them and fight against the desires of their lower natures. To the Galatians he gave a long list of nefarious behavior—which includes drinking bouts (*methe*). So serious is Paul about such life-styles that he adds that those who carry on in such ways will never inherit the Kingdom of God—implying that those who do these evil things are negating evidence that they are truly believers in Christ (Ga 5:16-21).

To the Ephesians, after upholding the glory of the church, Paul pleads that they as Christians live up to their calling by striving to behave appropriately—which behavior he describes in some detail over three chapters. He implores them to be sensible—not fools—and "not give way to drunkenness and dissipation that goes with it, but let the Holy Spirit fill you." Instead, he urges, "speak to one another in psalms, hymns and songs—make music in your hearts to the Lord" (Ep 5:19).

The church at Corinth, just west of Athens, seemed to be in continual crisis. Originally Paul had spent 18 months there preaching, teaching and organizing. He wrote them often and visited them at least twice after his first sojourn with them. The basic problem at Corinth was that as a crossroad of trade, it was a town with a lowlife element with lax moral standards which probably derived from the mixture of peoples and religions. Because of the trials and tribulations of the church there and Paul's subsequent concern for their spiritual growth, we are left with a wealth of guidance for the Christian life.

Paul's first letter to the Corinthians contains probably the best known and most used passage in all Christendom—that which gives instructions for observance of the Lord's Supper:

For the tradition which I handed on to you came to me from the Lord himself: that the Lord Jesus, on the night of his arrest, took bread and, after giving thanks to God, broke it and said: "This is my body, which is for you; do this as a memorial of me." In the same way, he took the cup after supper and said: "This cup is the new covenant sealed by my blood. Whenever you drink it, do this as a memorial of me." For every time you eat this bread and drink the cup, you proclaim the death of the Lord, until he comes (11:23-26).

These verses are in the middle of a discourse where Paul chides church members for their selfish manner as they shared—or didn't share—their food at the congregational potluck meals and for drinking so much wine before and during the repast they were too drunk to take part in the remembrance of the Lord's Supper! He tells them bluntly to eat at home and to examine themselves as to their worthiness to partake of the Lord's Supper.

It seems obvious that whatever the Corinthians were drinking was intoxicating, i.e., some form of wine. We can probably assume that after eating the communal meal at these get-togethers the Christians would have observed the Lord's Supper in the same manner as Jesus had done when he instituted this rite—using some of the beverage that had been served at the meal. Paul's point, however, was that the Lord's Supper should be celebrated decently, in order and by worthy participants.

Two other references to drunkenness in Paul's letters to the Corinthians contain much the same message as those to the Galatians and Ephesians. Both passages reflect the appalling character of the Corinthian society and the necessity for those professing to be Christians to be circumspect in their daily behavior. First, he admonishes them to have nothing to do with "so-called" Christians who lead loose lives, including drunkards (1 Co 5:11); second, he forcefully says that those who engage in certain wicked practices, which again includes drunkenness, will not gain access to the kingdom of God (1 Co 6:9-10).

These two passages are difficult to reconcile to current Christian thought which places emphasis on patience and forgiveness for wrongdoers, even within the church. (Paul said that, too, in Ep 4:32.) However, when we remember the low morality of the culture out of which the Corinthian believers came and which continued to surround them, we can understand Paul's forceful tone. He emphasized his conviction that anyone who continued to do the dreadful things he lists could not truly be saved! In other words, clean up your act to remove any doubt that you are a Christian!

To the Romans, Paul wrote adjuring them to "behave with decency: no revellings or drunkenness" because the day of deliverance is near (13:1-3). To the Thessalonians he writes similarly, admonishing them that because the Day of the Lord is approaching they must keep awake and sober (*nepho*) as children of the day in contrast to the sleepers (of the night)—drunkards who revel at night (1 Th 5:6-8). The implication of both these statements is that you just might miss the Great Day!

In four better known passages, Paul gives instruction regarding wine. The first, to the Romans, says that "it is good not to eat meat or drink wine *(oinos)* or do anything that makes your brother or sister stumble" (14:21). This admonishment comes at the conclusion of a passage in which Paul tells the church members not to hold in contempt someone who eats or does not eat what another feels is proper. Paul says, in effect, not to make rules to apply to everybody about eating or abstaining from specific foods. In other words, don't fall back into legalism. He then adds the verse quoted above—whose basis is consideration for one's neighbor!

The second well-known instruction is to Timothy, who evidently was having some digestive problems. Paul suggests he "take a little wine for your stomach's sake." Was the water suspect? Would the wine kill some bacteria or merely make Timothy feel better or perhaps be able to sleep? We do not know the pharmacopoeia of that day which produced this advice.

The third passage of counsel is included in both Paul's letters to Timothy and to Titus. In listing the qualifications for bishops and deacons, he says clearly that a bishop must be "no drinker" (*paroinos*) and "not given to strong drink" (1 Tm 3:3; Tt 1:17). The words sober and temperate here refer to being humbly self-controlled in all things, including drinking. To Timothy he adds that deacons should "not be addicted to much wine."

Finally, the rank and file church members are not ignored as he tells Titus how to organize the church in Crete, which again had to contend with a pagan culture. Paul instructs the older men to be sober and temperate, the older women to be reverent and not slaves to strong drink and the young women and men to be temperate in all things. Why older women were singled out in regard to strong drink, we don't know, but possibly the elderly widows found it often to be an escape from a life of loneliness and poverty. At any rate, persons of all ages are urged to be sober and temperate in order not to bring the church into disrepute.

Seven epistles in the New Testament were not written by Paul. Of those, only Peter mentions drunkenness. As he encourages the far-flung Christians to whom he writes to endure affliction, persecution and even death with which they are threatened because they are Christians, he tells them that as Christ endured bodily suffering and triumphed, they must and can do the same. Peter adjures them to demonstrate to all that they live for what God wills and thus are finished with sin—all the things they used to do in the pagan world: "license and debauchery, drunkenness (*oinophulgia*), revelry and tippling and the forbidden worship of idols" (1 P 4:3). He also implores them to be ready for whatever may come by living mentally stripped for action (1 P 1:13); to lead an ordered and sober life, given to prayer (1 P 4:7); and to be awake and on the alert for the enemy, the devil, who like a roaring lion prowls around looking for someone to devour. A graphic simile, indeed, for as this was written many Christians were literally facing lions in the public arena!

The Revelation of St. John, the last book in the New Testament canon, is a fascinating and variously interpreted account of John's apocalyptic vision of both current events of his time and future events. To explain these he uses many pictures and images, as did the prophets of the Old Testament, including the symbolism of wine, the winepress, grapes, vine and drunkenness. His imagery is both evidence that wine among the Bible people was considered a grace—a blessing from God—but as in the Old Testament, those things that are dearest to our hearts become judgments against us unless we elevate God to first place in our lives (6:6; 14:8, 10, 19; 16:19; 17:2, 6; 18:3, 13).

Conclusions

To make the question, What does the Bible say about drinking? cogent to our life, we must consider another question: What does the Bible say to us about *our* drinking?

Our first exercise starts by asking: How do we make up our minds what the Bible says for today on any subject? There are certain basic principles to consider:

1. What is the basic, overarching theme of the Bible?
2. What did specific events or lessons in Scriptures mean to the people when they occurred?
3. What do those incidents or messages mean to us today given our point in time and in light of the basic, overarching theme of the Scriptures?

In regard to the first principle, a succinct statement is found in the "Brief Statement of Belief" adopted by the Presbyterian Church (U.S.A.) in 1962 and which has served as a summary of the Reformed understanding of the Christian faith for the reunited Presbyterian church until a more expansive statement could be developed and incorporated into the *Book of Confessions*. It says: "The Bible as the written Word of God, sets forth what God has done and said in revealing [God's] righteous judgment and love, culminating in Christ."[29]

This statement is reminiscent of the Gospel of John prelude: "The Word became flesh and dwelt among us, full of grace and truth" (1:14 [RSV]). Jesus, the Word of grace, love and truth, interpreted God's message for us by bringing together two great fundamental commandments which until then had been held apart by the Jews. Christ

---

[29] "Brief Statement of Belief," *Book of Confessions,* Presbyterian Church, (U.S.A.) p. xiii, ¶1 of Appendix.

articulated this during the week before his crucifixion, when he answered the leading question of the lawyers (scribes) and theologians (Pharisees). The greatest commandment is, Jesus said,

"Hear O Israel: The Lord our God is the only Lord; love the Lord your God with all your heart, with all your soul, with all your mind and with all your strength." The second is this: "Love your neighbor as yourself." There is no other commandment greater than these! (Mk 12:29-31; cf. Dt 6:4; Lv 19:18b and Mt 22:39-40).

This then is the theme of the Scriptures—God's message which overarches, underlies and permeates our total relationship with God and with other human beings. What scope and power are in those words!

The second of our principles which tries to determine what a particular Scripture passage meant to the people involved when it happened, requires a study of their historical, religious and environmental milieu. Today we are fortunate to have easy access to many resources to help with such research.

The third principle involves comparing our situation with Biblical times, identifying differences or similarities in order to reach valid applications for today. As we relate our findings to Scriptural paradigms, we decide how these events or teachings direct the expression of our love and honor to God, to ourselves and to others.

After following this process thoughtfully, allowing as few preconceived ideas or prejudices as possible to inform our decision-making, the conclusions we reach should be reasonably reliable. Of course, infallibility is humanly impossible. New knowledge, discoveries and conditions bring new interpretations and solutions to both old and new problems, hence we can always anticipate new applications of the Scriptures.

But in applying these principles to our current subject, we can reflect on the Scriptural paradigms and relevant Biblical passages to determine what these passages mean to us today. Let us first consider the differences and then the similarities between those days and ours.

The Points of Difference

The most striking difference—which involves the use of alcohol—is no doubt technological. There was no automobile during Biblical times, let alone other sophisticated or dangerous types of machinery which are a routine part of our lives today. Transportation in Biblical times was largely by foot, camel, horse or donkey. Although awkward, perhaps tipsiness was not a great handicap in getting home—the animal was usually sober! Labor, also, was by human or animal brawn as opposed to our dependence on machinery—electronic and otherwise.

Another significant difference is the vast change in our societal organization. A great part of the world has moved from the ancient days of simple, homogeneous, tribal, usually agricultural communities which were largely self-contained and sustained to today's immense urban concentrations of people who, although very dependent on each other economically, live in stratified isolation. In addition, many of today's societies, like our own, are heterogenous mixtures of cultures, religions, races and national origins.

Confusion and lack of mores or guidelines reigns. Satisfying one's basic needs has become a complex operation which produces anxieties that must be coped with while looking for social and spiritual sustenance. Temptations aroused by advertisements and the easy access to alcohol and other drugs to ease these anxieties are found on every side.[30]

Several years ago, a missionary friend in Kenya wrote in reply to my question about the state of imbibing alcoholic beverages among the people with whom she worked. Her reply was illustrative of this issue. In former years, she wrote, when the people largely dwelt and worked in their villages in cooperative family units, alcohol was used, but it did not present the problem it had currently become. Whereas previously the villagers drank a home brew only on special occasions until their meager supply was exhausted, now, because of the urbanization of many of these villagers who work in factories, trades and governmental positions, and because of the commercial efforts of transnational liquor producers who vigorously promote and make their products available, it has become a regular habit of many men to

[30] Selden Bacon, "Alcohol and Complex Society," in *Society, Culture and Drinking Patterns*, ed. by D.J. Pittman and E.R. Snyder (New York: John Wiley and Sons, 1962) p. 78. This is splendid additional source.

stop at the bar on the way home from work. (The ubiquitous happy-hour!) Unfortunately, this hour often grows into the whole evening, so in contrast to a supply limited to what was produced in the village, the reserves of brew have become endless. The home life of these tipplers is affected—fathers see their children rarely, wives are saddled with additional work and responsibility. Disenchantment sets in and often results in broken homes. Sad to say, the conditions found in Kenya are hardly unique.

A third difference between biblical times and today revolves around the type of alcoholic beverage available. Historically, wine probably had an alcoholic content of ten to 17 percent, with the higher content constituting the Bible's "strong drink." Also, wine was routinely diluted with water by New Testament times. Drunkenness was possible with straight or strong wine, but with diluted drinks it probably produced other discomforts before inebriation took place. Today, wines are scientifically produced and controlled so that the usual alcohol strength is twelve to 17 percent, with some being fortified with more alcohol, like sherry which has as high as 21 percent. No one mixes wine with water today! Beer continues in the three to seven percent range with some going up to ten percent. Wine coolers and some "lite" beers have a lesser alcohol content.

In our culture the great difference comes in the introduction and commercialization of distilled liquors where the alcohol content is around 40 to 50 percent (80 to 100 percent proof).[31] Some drinkers prefer to take their whiskey "neat"—remember the frontier cowboys of the movies who drank glass after glass straight and seldom got drunk! Yet it is customary to dilute the product with water, ice, soda or other liquids to enhance (or cover) the taste, slow the inebriation or avoid burning a hole in the digestive tract. The bottom line remains that distillation produces a much stronger product which promises more inebriation for less volume.

Whether it was originally pushed commercially as a more profitable use of grain or as a guarantee of speedier drunkenness is a moot point. A "drink" according to current custom usually means distilled liquor in some form which is taken for its own sake rather than as a beverage with a meal—which exacerbates drinking problems. It is not news to anyone that the production of distilled liquors is a billion-dollar industry, jealously guarded and zealously advertised.

A final difference between biblical times and today is that alcohol has been supplanted as a medicinal element.

---

[31] Distillation was possibly invented by the Chinese before 2000 B.C. and improved on by the Arabs by 1700 B.C. It remained for the Europeans in the Middle Ages, notably the Irish, English and later the Scots, to popularize this method of increasing alcohol content. They brought this to America and eventually rum was supplanted by whiskey made from surplus grain. It was easier to ship whiskey than the grain itself, and certainly more profitable. The Whiskey Rebellion in 1740—a protest by whiskey-making farmers against higher taxes on their product—gave birth to "moonshining" enterprises—which still flourish to this day. See John A. Ewing and Beatrice A. Rouse, eds., *Drinking Alcohol in American Society—Issues and Current Research* (Chicago: Nelson-Hall, 1978) pp. 10-13.

In Bible days it was used as an anaesthetic, as an antiseptic for cleaning wounds, or was taken internally to alleviate discomfort, but today there are myriad drugs and medicines to do all of these, and more. Although some elixirs have alcohol in them, generally speaking the alcohol is not the chief active ingredient.

The Points of Similarity

People are still people. We find our roots in the first chapter of Genesis which explains the most basic facts of who we are. Adam and Eve, Cain and Abel and all the generations from theirs to ours have had the same basic needs, exhibited the same emotions, involved themselves in similar situations—good and bad—and tried to resolve them in much the same manner, even to the use of alcohol. Does alcohol answer a particular need? One author suggests "it must be suspected that even today [alcohol] serves a need better than anything else so far discovered."[32] What is that need and why do people drink alcohol to answer it?

The fact of the matter is that individuals usually drink for several reasons with little conscious thought about why—at least in the beginning. Some reasons reach back into one's cultural past, others are determined by one's milieu and some may be deeply psychological, or, as we now know, physiological. Here is a list of some

[32] Raymond Gerald McCarthy, ed., *Drinking and Intoxication* (Schenectady, NY: New College and University Press, 1959) p. 1.

reasons why people drink:

1. *It's there!*—the simplest reason. Like food on the table, one partakes of it. (Conversely, if it's not there, as during Prohibition, many do not drink it.)
2. *They like it and its effect,* which may be relaxation, escape and the promise of a good time.
3. However, imbibing what's there and liking it may well serve *deeper purposes,* according to Arnold Come. He says that many persons drink:
   • To find and maintain fellowship with other human beings—a fundamental human need. They want to know and be known by each other as unique persons and have found that a drink or two among friends in a home or tavern is the quickest way to establish rapport which wipes away the fog of human reserve and suspicion and allows them to open their hearts to each other.
   • To escape from the stress and strain of everyday life; to put to rest anxieties in regard to one's personal relationships, inner conflicts, repression, changes in life or worry about the meaning of it all.[33]
   • For self-discovery—to find out "who I am"; to find permission to be oneself—take off one's customary mask worn in everyday life.[34]
4. *Physiological compulsion,* in other words because one is an alcoholic. The seeming helplessness factor finally gave way to the recognition that compulsive drinking

---

[33] See also: Clinebell, pp. 71,72.
[34] Arnold B. Come, *Drinking: A Christian Position* (Philadelphia: Westminster Press, 1964) pp. 47-65.

has a physiological and genetic basis. The physiological processes involved are not well understood at this time; but it is becoming clear that there is an inherited propensity to alcoholism in families. Some alcoholics are addicted from the first drink and others drink for years before the mysterious line is crossed into compulsivity when one drinks because one has to—until help arrives and is accepted, or death occurs.

5. An interesting addendum to include in this section about people being people, is a list of why persons in the past and the present have chosen *not* to drink:
   - It's wrong, according to family, culture, religion.
   - Don't like the taste.
   - Want to maintain health and weight.
   - Want to be in charge mentally.
   - Had a bad experience with another's drinking.
   - Had a bad experience with own drinking.
   - Have other ways of having fun.
   - Have other ways of dealing with problems.
   - Pregnancy.
   - Persons in one's family are alcoholic.

We have now reached a watershed point where we must begin to determine what the Scriptures say to *us* about drinking. To recapitulate, we have found that:

1. Drinking wine for pleasure with meals or as a part of worship was normal in both the Old and New Testaments. It was considered a blessing from God and its absence symbolized God's displeasure.
2. Drunkenness was never acceptable.
3. There is no overall condemnation of drinking alcoholic

beverages in the Bible.

4. There are many similarities concerning drinking in Biblical times and today, but there are also significant differences between then and now.

5. There is little direct, transferable instruction in the Bible concerning our drinking today.

So we find ourselves with helpful insights, but still with no definite answer to our question regarding what the Bible says to us about our drinking. Dr. Hewitt articulates the problem well when he asks, "Is it enough to merely note that moderate drinking was allowed in the biblical world?"[35]

He concludes not, for much the same reasons of similarities and differences we have already listed. In addition, it would seem that if we were to leave this question about the permissibility or advisability of drinking at this juncture, we could justifiably be accused of saying: "Drinking alcoholic beverages is o.k.—the Bible says so—go to it!"

Emphatically I hope that we see that such a conclusion is not the answer to the question. While we are trying to be honest in understanding what the Bible says, we remain overwhelmingly aware of the many implications and complexities which shroud such a simplistic statement in today's world.

Therefore, let us now find what the Bible says *indirectly* as we relate our relevant findings to the over-arching theme of the Scriptures as Jesus summarized it

---

[35] Hewitt, p. 20.

in the first and second greatest commandments:

- Loving God,
- Loving Others,
- Loving Ourselves.

After having done this conscientiously, we will be able to make a cogent statement in answer to the basic question about our use of alcoholic beverages.

Loving God

We are told we must love and honor God with all our hearts (emotion), minds (intellects), souls (spirit) and strength (endurance) (Mk 12:29-30). What does this prime requirement mean in regard to drinking or not drinking alcohol?

Using Scripture to interpret Scripture, we are adjured to:

1. Not let any other thing come before God in our lives (Ex 20:3); therefore we cannot make an idol of our fondness for alcohol, our desire to be socially acceptable or make a profit at the expense of the well-being of others.

2. Recognize that all God has created is intrinsically good, and it is our duty and privilege to use God's gifts in a manner which glorifies God (Gn 1:29-31; 1 Tm 4:4). This includes:
   - "Keep sober, upright and Godly" (Tt 2:11-13 [RSV]; Rm 13:13; 1 Th 5:6-8; 1 P 1:13)—sober meaning temperate, moderate, cool-headed in all things.

This definition is the key to our imbibing alcoholic beverages. None of us has difficulty condemning drunkenness as the Bible does; the question for us is whether we can remain temperate, moderate, cool-headed in all things while we imbibe alcohol?

- Strive to honor God in daily life both for the sake of the purity of the church and also for the sake of its witness in the world (1 Co 5:9-13; 6:9-11). As Christians we are not free to do as we please—our bodies are a shrine for the indwelling of the Holy Spirit, therefore we should honor God in our outward, visible behavior (1 Co 6:19,20). It is a serious matter for us Christians when God's will clashes with our will or our inner desires which are often born of societal norms. It is often difficult to find strength to say "no" to cultural pressure in order to honor God in our behavior. Drinking in today's society certainly falls into this arena of jousting.
- All believers are to live circumspectly for the sake of God and the church, but the leaders, elders, bishops and deacons, in addition, must measure up to a long list of specific qualifications given in I Timothy 3:2-13. Among these specifications are that they be "sober, temperate . . . not given to drink or a brawler" (v. 3), and Titus 1:7 repeats that they be "no drinker, no brawler." In both passages the Greek word for drink / drinker is *paroinas*. It means to be taken over by a love for, or having a predilection for wine—possibly be addicted. The standards set by Paul are stiff and apply today as much as they did in the first century.

In my own church experience I have heard this list of

qualifications read several times, but I have never heard any discussion about the drinking requirement as nominees were chosen for various church offices. Is this because it is assumed that a church member, otherwise eligible for office, would not be overtaken with drink, or does it indicate an ignorance of the signs of preoccupation with drinking, or is it because it doesn't matter?

3. "Let the Holy Spirit fill you"—do not rely on "drinking and the dissipation that goes with it" to produce ecstasy, but "speak to one another in psalms, hymns and songs: sing and make music in your hearts to the Lord . . ." (Ep 5:18-20) which can, indeed, produce "highs". Among the happiest memories of my youth are the "sings" we had in church and homes. Who has not been thrilled by the whole-hearted singing of a joyous congregation? There are many other, often simple, ways to relax and have a good time so this advice to be filled with the Holy Spirit as opposed to being filled with alcohol is not to be taken lightly by the Christian. The two are not mutually accommodating. Anderson Spickard says in his book that heavy drinking is very serious because it quenches spiritual understanding—"their spirituality is devoid of power."[36]

Loving Others

We must love our neighbors—our fellow human-beings—as we love ourselves. The essence of Christianity

[36] Anderson Spickard, M.D. and Barbara R. Thompson, *Dying for a Drink* (Waco, TX: Word Books, 1985) p. 44.

is that not only should God be central in our lives, but also that our love for others should be the central expression of our faith—our rule of life (I Jn 4:7-12, 17, 19; 2 Jn 6). What does such a rule say about drinking?

Since we have repeatedly read in Scripture that the believer must be sober and temperate in life-style and since we know from general knowledge and experience the effect of alcohol on the mind, body and behavior, we should not have difficulty outlining a rule of life that avoids careless, unloving use of alcoholic beverages.

Points to consider:

1. Remembering the discussion of "differences," we can graphically see how even moderate drinking today can affect others, notably when we drive automobiles, boats or airplanes, or operate any machine. Once I heard an officer of the California Highway Patrol say that he thought drivers who had only a drink or two which produced a blood alcohol level (BAL) of .03 percent or .05 percent, were the most dangerous because their impaired skill and judgment was not evident, yet was often coupled with exuberant self-confidence, or worse, sleepiness. Adding these cases to those legally under the influence (.10 percent BAL),[37] it is frightening when one realizes how many dangerous drivers are on our highways and the horrendous extent to which injuries and fatalities—our own and others—impinge on many additional persons.

2. Another significant difference arises because of our

[37] Many states are now lowering the BAL (Blood Alcohol Level) to .08%. Canada and all European nations have .08% or lower.

tightly knit modern society where individual behavior affects a widening circle in the same way as a sonic boom reverberates through space until it finally assaults our ears with its deafening bang. Imprudent use of alcohol by individuals or groups sorely strains relationships in the same manner as judgment becomes hazy, efficiency declines, bonds are warped, costs mount and violence and criminal behavior (including white-collar crime) are facilitated. Those affected range from family and friends through employer-employee relationships, community groups, including the church, to those in government—local, national and international. We will probably never know how much we are all affected by over-imbibing in high governmental circles or by pressures exerted on our legislators by the alcohol beverage industry.

3. Because it is specifically important in relationships with others, we bring up again the injunctions of Romans 14:21: "It is good not to eat meat or drink wine or do anything that makes your brother or sister stumble" [NRSV]. Attempts are often made to make this passage, dubbed the "weaker-member verse," stand on its own as a legalistic prohibition against drinking, especially when read with 1 Corinthians 8:1-13 which deals with eating food consecrated to idols. Yet Paul was clear in saying this was not to be a new law. Like the Romans, we are no longer under the law! Rather our behavior should be the natural result of acting in freedom and love toward others as Christ commanded. On some occasions and for some persons this may well mean abstinence in consideration for others. For those not choosing abstinence, it at least means thoughtfulness and care regarding drinking

alcohol. Examples of when to exercise such care include thinking about:

- drinking before driving (autos, motorcycles, boats, planes, buses, trains).
- serving alcohol when children and young people are present.
- allowing it to be served at teen-age parties.
- "pushing" drinks on guests.
- serving other types of liquid refreshments instead of or in addition to alcoholic beverages.
- respecting others' decisions about drinking.

In his discussion of Romans 14:21, John Spahr gives a personal example which illustrates the spirit of this verse:

This writer [John Spahr] is an alcoholic and he chooses to abstain out of necessity, for alcohol can no longer appear on his diet. It is that simple. My wife, "B.J.", who is not an alcoholic, chooses to abstain completely, lest her drinking would cause me to "stumble" (the alcoholics call it "slip"). Alcohol is my weakness not hers. That is love . . . Our children have learned from that example, our married daughters and their husbands and our son, choose to drink in their life-styles; but as an act of love, choose never to bring it into our home nor serve it when we are in theirs. That is a beautiful application of the spirit of this Scripture and that is love. Not law, but love.[38]

---

[38] Spahr, pp. 73-74.

In reflecting on this example, one would have to agree that this is not only a loving but a quite possible act of love on the part of a family. A recovering alcoholic by no means expects everyone or every event to be alcohol free, but it should be possible in one's family circle.

This is an appropriate point at which to speak about wine being used in observance of the Lord's Supper—a matter of discussion in many Protestant churches. Good scholarship indicates that fermented wine was served at the original Last Supper; also, tradition, based on that first event, dictates the use of fermented wine in many churches, e.g., Catholic—both Roman and Eastern branches, Episcopal and some other Protestant groups. In the United States, some Protestant denominations (e.g., Methodist, Presbyterian, Congregational, Baptist) began to use unfermented grape juice during the Temperance Movement of the 19th and early 20th centuries and many have not returned officially to the use of wine.

Among some of these churches presently there is argument for returning to tradition and this has persuaded some churches to start to do so. However this is not the case in all of the historically abstinent churches or in the more conservative evangelical or fundamentalist churches. In the ambivalent group is the Presbyterian church which has stated that wine may be used but those who do not wish to take it should be able to do so easily and without judgment by having grape juice served also. Still, throughout the United States in a great many Protestant churches, unfermented grape juice continues to be served in a spirit of tradition which appears quite well established to most current members; and perhaps in kindness to those who may be addicted to alcohol.

In Roman Catholic and Episcopal churches, provision is now made for alcoholic priests and parishioners to abstain from actually drinking the wine. Some alcoholic priests believe God gives special grace to those who do take a sip so that their addiction will not be activated; others continue to abstain rather than be sorry.

Resolving this difference of opinion and practice in a sensible manner is a good example of reconciling the Scripture passages with current knowledge in regard to the use of alcohol. It also is a prime example of considering others—in love.

Although most church members rarely think of this problem, I have never forgotten how this issue became engraved on my consciousness. Twenty years ago I participated in a weekend spiritual retreat on the historic island of Iona off the Western coast of Scotland. On Sunday morning the retreaters worshipped in an ages-old church in that historic setting. The service concluded with Communion. After receiving the bread individually, a chalice was passed for each person to sip. When it was passed to me I noted that it was a very pungent wine whose aroma assaulted the nostrils as one partook.

Later that afternoon, I went strolling around the island and through the tiny village where I came upon my roommate, a fairly young woman, sitting on the post office steps. I sat down beside her to rest a bit and then noted she was quite agitated. We had not talked together a great deal up to that time, but I felt compelled to ask what was bothering her.

With hesitancy, she told me she had never taken

Communion. Although she had been born and reared a Scottish Presbyterian, albeit a rebellious one, she had had little to do with the church until the past year when she had a genuine conversion experience. She was at this retreat to learn more about living the Christian life.

I expressed surprise that she had never taken Communion. With this the dam broke! She told me she was an alcoholic who had found safety and sobriety when she was rescued from a very dangerous situation by a Christian mission worker. She had had many similar experiences which had brought her close to death on more than one occasion. Now she was living by her faith in God and with the help of AA.

But how was she to handle the Communion? She wanted to partake, but that morning just whiffing the wine as she passed the cup to the next person was almost more than she could bear. Now she was wrestling in her soul as she sat there. We talked for quite awhile and I shared my sister's story. I also assured her that God understood her situation and would certainly understand her not taking the wine in the Communion service. After simple prayer, we walked back to the retreat house. I have often wondered where she is now. . . .

That experience occurred just before I became involved in alcohol ministry, but it left two indelible impressions in my mind: first, we have no idea who or where there may be an alcoholic person trying desperately to live a sober life; and second, plain grape juice—verily the fruit of the vine—has ample significance in the observance of the Lord's Supper.

This brings us to the last point to consider in the

matter of loving and caring for others:

4. Can we love and care about those who are already afflicted with or affected by problems with alcohol, remembering that just as God loves us, we must love:
   - a boozing parent or parents, perhaps on welfare, unable to care for home and children, or
   - the drunk driver who causes a fatal accident, or
   - the over-imbibing clown who spoils the party, or
   - the spouse who won't admit a drinking problem, or
   - the disobedient, wilful teenage drinker, or
   - the weekend binger who bullies / beats his wife, or
   - the bothersome neighbor woman with the bleary eyes and smeary make-up, or
   - the over-confident boss with wandering hands after a three martini lunch, or
   - the employee who botches sales over the same type lunch, or
   - the behavior-problem child, perhaps from an alcoholic home, who wants to play with your child, or acts out in your class, or
   - the smelly, dirty, homeless person passed out in the vacant store doorway.

Here are four practical guidelines to help us exercise this love:

1. Realize that it can, indeed, be difficult to love, but God is with us and in us (1 Jn 4:19).
2. Be willing to let God change our attitudes.
3. Maintain our humility, for "there but for the grace of God go I."

4. Do actively what we can in prevention and treatment, even while we learn.[39]

Dr. Hewitt sums it up well:

Questions about the use of alcohol and drugs are not resolved by citing this or that text, but by the more difficult struggle of asking as Luther put it, what it means to be "Christ to my neighbor," what it means to be a loving servant in the 20th century"[40] [and the 21st!].

Loving Ourselves

To be a loving servant, we must love ourselves. To acknowledge loving ourselves deliberately, let alone work toward such regard, is very difficult for many. As Christians we are taught to think first of other persons, to share, to build others up and not to think too highly of ourselves. Modern psychology has prompted us to see that we must value ourselves as God values us in order to be full, useful and happy persons. Christian counselors strive to help us learn to love ourselves by nurturing,

---

[39] Exercising love for those afflicted and affected does not mean exoneration for those who harm themselves or others while in their cups, but it does mean extending understanding, one human being to another, even when necessarily severe penalties are levied by the courts or when other suffering comes as a natural consequence of the misbehavior. In fact, facing-up and paying the penalty, coupled with the help of a caring person may well bring such transgressors to deal with their drinking problems.

[40] Hewitt, p. 30.

forgiving, rejoicing, understanding and sharing ourselves. This is good theology as well as good psychology for valuing ourselves is basic to valuing others.

As in all relationships, loving ourselves incurs responsibilities toward ourselves. This also is true in regard to the use of alcoholic beverages. Thus our aim is not only to help us understand what the Bible says about drinking such beverages, but also to help us make deliberate, educated and loving decisions about our personal use of alcohol.

Paul's epistles are full of suggestions about making decisions. In 1 Corinthians where he writes about living as a Christian, he says, " 'I am free to do anything,' you say. Yes, but not everything is for my good. No doubt I am free to do anything, but I for one will not let anything make free with me" (6:12).

This passage is particularly apropos in regard to using alcohol, for careless or constant over-imbibing can take over a person's life—as a recovering alcoholic will readily tell you.

Following are some factors to consider when making a decision about personal alcohol use:

1. Where am I now in the matter of drinking: Why do I want to or not want to? If I do, do any of the reasons listed under "why people drink" (pp. 84-86) apply? Do I know how it affects my behavior? Do I have limits? If I do not drink, do I know why? Am I comfortable with my position?
2. Do I have factual knowledge of alcohol itself and its effects on the body and the mind?

3. How does my drinking or not drinking affect others?
4. What is my genetic background? Are there any alcoholics or heavy drinkers at present or in previous generations of my family?
5. Do I grasp the spiritual implications in regard to the use of alcohol?
6. Do I drink before I drive? Can I afford liquor? What does advertising mean to me? Can I stand on my own feet, resisting peer pressure?
7. *For young people:* Am I old enough according to the law to drink?

To feel alcohol is necessary in any degree (in contrast to the complete dependency of alcoholism) is cheating oneself of the fullness of life. In an excellent United Methodist adult education lesson booklet which includes a series on responsibility in regard to the use of drugs and alcohol, the author paraphrases an opinion given by Clinebell saying, "Alcoholism and other addictions are essentially results of unlived lives. The unlived life or the unused potential for life is a common thread that seems to run through the stories of all alcoholics."[41]

Recently, a T.V. miniseries portrayed the life of Barbara Hutton, the granddaughter of F.W. Woolworth. She inherited his vast fortune in the 1920s—and became known as "the poor little rich girl." Hers was a story of childhood rejection and a life that was hollow. What positive inner resources she might have had were

[41] Patricia Merrill, "Alcohol and Other Drugs," in *Faith Meets Life Series,* ed. by John P. Gilbert (Nashville: United Methodist Publishing House, 1981) pp. 44-45.

squelched by supercilious companions and a frivolous life-style. Eventually, she trusted no one, loved no one but her son and felt no one, including herself, loved her. Her unsatisfying life was filled with dependence on drugs and alcohol. She went from party to party, house to house and husband to husband and died broke and broken—a prime example of an empty, unlived sad life!

Whether Barbara Hutton ever had an opportunity to hear and accept God's love and thus find herself truly loved and able to give love, we do not know. Those who have heard the Message can fully live a real life, independent of chemical props—or wealth—knowing they are God's temple where the spirit of God lives.

Finally . . .

What does the Bible say about the use, or more specifically *our* use of alcoholic beverages? It seems evident that in spite of the lack of specific instructions in the Bible, if we are earnest we cannot escape considering our use of alcohol in this day and age. The seriousness of drunkenness still holds and, if anything, it is more serious in our day. The casual social use of alcohol must be weighed carefully in all its aspects in order to avoid the deleterious effects of careless imbibing. Abstinence is fully desirable—and is practiced by at least a third of all Americans. "Responsible drinking" (for the lack of a better term) is a permissible option, but the parameters of such drinking must be well understood and consistently observed. The real key is to know that we do have a choice!

Alcoholism is in another category. Defined as a disease, the responsibility for individuals who have alcoholism in their families is to "take it easy" or preferably abstain. Everyone should avoid heavy drinking. Furthermore, all persons should have a knowledge of alcoholism so it can be recognized (even though alcoholics will usually deny it) and help can be offered to both the victims and their families.

Compassion—with knowledge and discipline—must be extended to those caught in problems with alcohol, as we are bidden to do in regard to all persons caught painfully in the quandaries of living. As the Apostle Paul says:

> Adapt yourselves no longer to the pattern of this present world, but let your minds be remade and your whole nature thus transformed. Then you will be able to discern the will of God and know what is good, acceptable and perfect (Rm 12:2).

6

The "Spiritual Dimension" ❖

In the chapter on what the Bible says, we touched on the importance of the spiritual aspect of alcohol problems. This is such an important dimension or "angle," as AA people are wont to say, I would like to discuss it more fully. Since we in the church are in the spiritual business, it is important we have a clear picture of this facet and are also able to express it reasonably well. We need to see our ministry encompassing alcohol problems as a natural part of the church's mission.

From my years of working in this area, I have come to see—as have many others—that wellness or unwellness has a definite spiritual relationship. Beyond this, I have discovered from much conversation with recovering alcoholics and others involved in alcohol problems that the development of the spiritual life is uniquely important both in prevention and treatment.

Unfortunately there is a dearth of material available in simple, understandable terms which explains what such a spiritual connection in regard to alcohol problems should be. Some speakers and writers touch on the subject, many recovering alcoholic persons know it well from experience, but appear at a loss for words or terms to explain it. It would seem to me that this discussion need not be exhaustive theologically, scripturally or experientially, but it should lay out in simple terms, as it applies to the issues surrounding alcohol, what is meant by *spiritual* and *spirituality* and the related terms, *religion* and *religious*.

When dealing with this aspect of alcoholism, I personally have had to draw upon a wide range of resources for help. But the experiences I have had through the years in hearing, reading, digesting, discussing and living in (or departing from) the guidance of the Holy Spirit is my chief resource.

Spirit → Spiritual / Spirituality

Within each of us is a real, but mysterious something which we define as the spirit—or the soul. We all know we have it. It is that mystical something which gives us life, enables us to commune with each other and is that which C.S. Lewis says underlies a sense of right and wrong in relation to each other.[42] Most importantly, it is that which reaches out beyond ourselves seeking oneness with the greater Spirit which we sense is all about us. It is that which makes us human beings, alive and lively, and which echoes deep in our being the awe, love, joy, peace and warmth during the good times in life and which triggers anguish when we suffer sadness, weariness, anger, remorse or guilt. Our spirit also causes us to rebel in indignation at unfairness.

Most of the time we are not overtly conscious of this spiritual component in ourselves. When things are going well, we take it for granted, as we do our physical bodies while in good health. However, if either begins to give us pain, we pay attention! Deep-hurting spiritual pain is often more difficult to bear than physical pain. In such circumstances—remembering fleetingly the good-times—we cry out: "What's it all about? Why do these awful things happen? Why do they happen to *me*? Why can't life always be good? How can I endure it? What's the point—the meaning of life anyway? We crave answers and search through our own experience and that of others, finding little satisfaction. In desperation, and perhaps illogically to some, we call on the unknown: that greater something which seemingly pervades and surrounds our existence.

Throughout the ages those who have searched and believe they have found an answer to such questions feel

---

[42] *Mere Christianity* (New York: Macmillan Company, 1960) Ch. 1. He calls it the "Law of Human Nature."

fortunate, indeed. According to their newfound understanding the jigsaw pieces of life and living begin to come together and fit into the scheme of things because communication is established between the human spirit and the greater, all-powerful Spirit which is perceived to be around all, in all, yet beyond all. In becoming aware of this newly found spiritual reality—plugging-in, as it were—the option of letting this power source dominate and direct one's life is presented to each discoverer. This, in simple and general terms, is the genesis of conscious spiritual life sought by people from the beginning, defined and manifested in many different ways by countless peoples through the ages.

For Christians, this spiritual life begins when our spirits answer affirmatively the invitation offered by the all-powerful, all-knowing and all-present God who through Jesus Christ, the Revealer, says, "Come unto Me." To find this spiritual life is to rejoice with St. Augustine, who in A.D. 346 after his early life of sin and searching, learned of the God of the Christians and accepted the proffered redemption and reconciliation through Christ. In his famous *Confessions* he wrote, "Thou movest us to delight in praising Thee; for thou hast formed us for Thyself, and our hearts are restless till they find rest in Thee."[43] In our hearts many centuries later we shout, "Amen and amen!"

The message—the Gospel—which Augustine heard and

---

[43] David Otis Fuller, ed., *Confessions of St. Augustine* (Grand Rapids, MI: Zondervan, 1947) p. 19.

accepted and by which he lived the remaining years of his life was that which the Apostle Paul had written about 300 years earlier in his letter to the Galatians when he said that after having received the Holy Spirit through accepting the Gospel message, the fruits of the Spirit (meaning the Holy Spirit, the operative power and guide) were possible, namely: "love, joy, peace, patience, kindness, goodness, fidelity, gentleness and self-control" (5:22). What a harvest!

Even though in our humanity we will never produce perfect fruits, such as we do produce with the aid of the Spirit will bring us and others joy and happiness above and beyond that which we thought possible. The next two verses in this Epistle are apropos to the general subject of this book: "And those who belong to Christ Jesus have crucified the lower nature with its passions and desires. If the Spirit is the source of our life, let the Spirit also direct our course" (5:24-25). This is the spiritual life or Christian spirituality.

The core theme here is that it is vital for the recovering alcoholic to have a true spiritual life activated—or reactivated—nurtured and lived daily in order to conquer the overwhelming craving for alcohol. The alcoholic who, like the rest of us, is basically searching for spiritual wholeness somehow begins to use alcohol in seeking answers to the problem areas of life or to avoid answering the despairing questions of life. Clinebell says: "for the alcoholic, religion and alcohol often are functionally interchangeable."[44] Thus if alcoholics are rid of their euphoric crutches, they must find meaningful answers in some other way. Finding and living a new and real spiritual life is the key to finding and maintaining a sober life. This is the same spiritual message entrusted to those who have already found it and are in the church. It is the one they are commissioned to share diligently, but somehow have largely missed sharing with alcoholics and their families.

It is also the message of AA. For members of this unique history-making fellowship, the spiritual life begins when they declare their lives to be unmanageable (Step One of AA)[45] and turn over their wills and lives to God as they understood God (Step Three).[46] These simple phrases coming out of the experience of the intrepid founding members over 50 years ago, enable men and women, whether young or old, learned, uneducated or in-between, who are desolate, miserable, humble or humbled, to begin their spiritual journey of recovery with God—the Power greater than themselves.

Dr. Ernest Kurtz in his book, *Not-God, A History of Alcoholics Anonymous,* points out that the first three steps of AA, in effect, represent conversion or salvation

---

[44] Clinebell, p. 154.

[45] See Appendix for a complete list of the Twelve Steps of AA.

[46] Some critics say that the concept of "God as we understood Him" (the past tense comes from the steps having been written by the founders, Bill W. and Dr. Bob, after they had experienced them in their recovery) is too limiting, even sacrilegious, but I think not. Do we not all come to God in the understanding we have of God at that moment—as little children—and then grow?

and surrender, all definitely Christian concepts.[47] They are followed by steps four through twelve which prescribe cleansing and strengthening activity which confirms that the conversion-surrender is genuine. The whole experience is spoken of in Step Twelve as a "spiritual awakening." In actuality, many persons coming to AA at first do not understand and some resist the concept of a Higher Power, but gradually by "working the program," a genuine spiritual awakening occurs, often quietly, but nevertheless in a bona fide manner.

The following quote from the "Big Book," *Alcoholics Anonymous,* indicates a parallel truth and profundity to St. Augustine's statement quoted earlier:

> The great fact is just this, and nothing less: That we have had deep and effective spiritual experiences which revolutionized our whole attitude toward life, toward our fellows and toward God's universe. The central fact of our lives is the absolute certainty that our Creator has entered into our hearts and lives in a way which is indeed miraculous. He has commenced to accomplish things for us which we could never do by ourselves.[48]

We see how an alcoholic may perhaps become a Christian, but what do we say to the casual observer who asks:

---

[47] Ernest Kurtz, *Not-God, A History of Alcoholics Anonymous* (Center City, MN: Hazelden) p. 182, ff.

[48] *Alcoholics Anonymous,* the "Big Book," 3rd Ed. (New York: Alcoholics Anonymous World Services, Inc., 1976) p. 25.

- How can persons who say they already are Christians be alcoholics?
- How can they hurt people so deliberately?
- Degrade themselves so?
- Do they not have the desire to do better?
- Why doesn't God help them?
- Are they really Christians?
- What do we do about *them*?

The not so simple answer is that the propensity to develop the disease of alcoholism is no respecter of persons and can be activated into full-blown alcoholism with the ingestion of alcohol—which is plentiful and okay to drink in our society even by believers / Christians / church-members if they wish. In time, alcoholic Christians realize during fleeting, sober moments that they are hurting their loved ones, but like most alcoholics they usually manage to blame others or their situation—and continue to drink.

During such fleeting moments, alcoholics often want to do better and want God to help them. They may even quit for awhile, but they can't make it. They must have their alcohol! Chances are their families and friends will deny they are alcoholics—good church members (or pastors) can't possibly be alcoholics! This enables them to continue in their alcoholism—as my friend Dorene did. Moreover, when pastors are alcoholics, it is not uncommon for their congregations to deny the drinking problems, even when the signs are obvious. One recovering alcoholic priest I know had a bishop who pooh-poohed the idea that the priest was an alcoholic—which forced the priest to turn to an outside source for help! (Ordained clergy have one of the highest rates of alcoholism among the professions.)

What has happened? Have these alcoholics lost their souls' salvation? The answer is certainly not! Is the salvation of a believer who has schizophrenia, diabetes, Alzheimer's or brain-tumor in danger? The answer here is obvious. However the problem with alcoholic Christians is that their spiritual life recedes far into the background (a concomitant condition which aggravates the disease).

Spickard says in his book:

> Long before a heavy drinker becomes an alcoholic, his relationship with God is badly damaged. Heavy drinking quenches spiritual understanding and often leads the drinker to violate his own moral principles. . . . For the alcoholic, the moral damage never ends. He repeatedly violates his own sense of right and wrong by telling petty lies, cheating at work, hiding bottles, stealing and verbally or physically abusing other members of his family. . . . However, twisted and unpredictable the actions of the alcoholic become, his conscience is never fully soluble in alcohol. He is aware of his moral corruption and he is tormented by guilt.[49]

The Apostle Paul understood this struggle when he wrote to the Romans about the battle between wanting to do the right thing, yet failing to do it. "O miserable

---

[49] Spickard, p. 43.

creature that I am!" he cried out (7:24).

I cannot shake the pain which overwhelmed me at the memorial service a few months ago for a bright, personable, loving man who had been a good father, son and husband; an elder in his church for several years; and highly regarded at his work. All were stunned to learn that at the prime age of 42 years, he had shot himself one afternoon just before Thanksgiving because he could not tolerate his hellish addiction to alcohol and the mess it was making in his life. Through a lack of understanding on the part of many and the bungled help offered him and his family, he had been unable to find long-term sobriety with its renewed spiritual strength and joy.

For alcoholic Christians who do find genuine help—and many do—it is necessary to return to square one in their Christian faith—take AA's Step One, declaring their lives unmanageable and throwing themselves on God for healing and rebuilding their lives.

We need also to remember the families of alcoholics who also suffer agonies of body, mind and spirit—a state now popularly referred to as "co-dependency." A serene, sane, even joyful spiritual life is available to them on the same terms, even when the alcoholics they are related to will not face-up to their problem. Support groups such as Al-Anon, Alateen and Adult Children of Alcoholics are built on AA principles and are tremendously helpful. Found in most communities, such groups deal with various needs and help family members climb out of the black hole of confusion and despair by finding hope through talking with others who have experienced the same agonies and are conquering them.

Of course, the local church congregation can be the ultimate support group if its members are knowledgeable, open and alert to recognizing and helping families (inside and outside the church) caught in this situation. Love, understanding and practical assistance extend the spirit of Christ as healing, wisdom and strength for coping is imparted to suffering family members.

❧ ❧ ❧

In general, the words "spiritual and spirituality" are often used interchangeably with "religion and religious." Yet AA members are fond of saying their program is "spiritual, not religious." Why do they say this? Following is an explanation:

Out of the human search for and discovery of the spiritual life comes religion, which simply put is the codification of tenets, traditions and ethics established in an effort to maintain an ongoing spiritual life and values. These practices tend to become formalized as they are passed down from generation to generation, sometimes with little understanding. From time to time, there is a probing and a rethinking of the tenets and traditions which can result in reformation or sometimes the establishing of new and separate entities. This ebb and flow occurs in all major religions.

Just so have there been changes in the Christian religion which grew from spiritual roots in the Old Testament and became reality in the coming of Jesus Christ and the establishment of the Christian church. From its beginning, there have been countless vicissitudes in organization, doctrinal statements, visible and invisible ritual and traditions, separations and joinings, but the basic tenets have not changed. As a result, we see today many complex and influential church bodies, large and small, which strive to share and maintain the spiritual message which gave them birth.

Although, as modern Christians we enjoy much of the ritual and tradition of today's churches, we know that we must continually work to keep the spiritual message in the forefront, reaching out to those who are in need. Most churches have this as their goal and there are many faithful believers, alive in the Spirit, who pray and work toward accomplishing this goal both through spoken testimony and acts of love and caring. However there are, unfortunately, missed opportunities and areas of need, questionable cultural influences and other superficialities masquerading as religion which can discourage those who seek a direct and simple message.

This then may be the crux of the argument between "spiritual and religious," between the simplicity of the spiritual message vs. the often perceived superficiality or negativism experienced by some alcoholics and their families in the church milieu. AA appeals through its simple, to-the-point fellowship of love and caring. However, given that out of the discovery of the spiritual connection within and beyond ourselves, comes religion, is it valid for the church or AA to exclude each other? Can each not benefit by understanding the other? Church members can learn about alcoholism and the importance of spirituality in the recovery process, reach out to afflicted persons and welcome them and AA groups into their churches just as AA members can find added joy, strength and growth—as well as friends—by participating in a church. An added bonus is that AA folk can become effective educators in a congregation in regard to alcohol problems.

Thus I question the usefulness of the statement: "spiritual not religious." It seems rather that we should differentiate between spirituality and "religiosity," the latter being defined as an ostentatious, superficial practice of religion. Dr. Kurtz says we should more properly differentiate between "spiritual or religious" and "churchy."[50] The latter perhaps suggests a major emphasis on culturally acceptable but perhaps empty conformity in ritual, thinking and behavior. So spiritual / spirituality and religious / religion are two sides of the same coin. Our mission is to keep both sides clean and shining so the value of the coin can be readily seen!

Surely Alcoholics Anonymous has proven to be a remarkable fellowship which pioneered modern interest and recovery from alcoholism. As far as can be determined, it holds the highest rate of alcoholics maintaining sobriety. AA's principles dominate the alcoholism treatment world. However, there are recovering alcoholics who do not go to AA for various reasons. There are good and viable programs involving group therapy—some of which emphasize the spiritual message even more strongly than AA. A few individuals go it alone, but this is usually difficult. The complexity of the disease virtually demands

[50] Kurtz, p. 177.

help and emphasis on the spiritual / mystical relationship of oneself to God and others.

I believe it is necessary to be respectful and grateful for the recovery of alcoholics by whatever means! Let what works, work!

7

"Alcohol Abuse vs. Alcoholism" ❖

There seems to be widespread misunderstanding regarding the terms *alcohol abuse* and *alcoholism*.[51] Both are used interchangeably often, but a distinction should be drawn because they are not fully synonymous.[52] The differences in these terms needs to

---

[51] It is important to remember that of the 70 percent of Americans who drink, only one in 10 are alcoholic—about 11.2 million. However, out of the remainder, it is estimated there are another ten million non-alcoholic, occasional or chronic abusers. The balance we optimistically hope are unharmed and harmless moderate drinkers!

[52] Mark Keller, Mairi McCormick and Vera Efron, *A Dictionary of Words about Alcohol,* 2nd Ed. (New Brunswick, NJ: Rutgers Center of Alcohol Studies, 1982) p. 14, suggests that "alcohol abuse" is used "possibly with other meanings or to avoid commitment to a specific

be emphasized, for "alcohol abuse" is in many ways the larger problem as it touches us in many subtle ways.

The confusion in respect to these terms is not surprising when one reads the available literature or gleans information about alcohol problems from other sources.

Beginning in the last century, when alcohol was popularly considered the villain, e.g., "demon rum," *it* caused the problems. In the United States, the Volstead Act—Prohibition—was the logical result of such a concept. However, when that effort proved less than successful, some minds began to perceive that the persons imbibing the alcohol might be the problem, not alcohol.

After Repeal in 1933, serious analysis of the problems brought about by drinking began. Even after alcoholism began to be recognized as a disease in all its complexities, a new confusion arose. Dr. E.M. Jellinek, (1890-1963) considered the originator of modern alcoholism research and who established the Yale Center of Alcohol Studies in 1940 (which later became the Rutgers Center of Alcohol Studies), stated that alcoholism is "any use of alcoholic beverages that causes any damage to the individual or society."[53] He then proceeded to break alcoholism down into five types—which illustrate why this scholar and pioneer unwittingly also contributed to the confusion. Jellinek captioned his findings with Greek letters—a nomenclature still in vogue:

meaning or from uncertainty about the nature or condition thus labeled." Such an obfuscatory use is not intended here in any way!

[53] E. M. Jellinek, *The Disease Concept of Alcoholism* (Highland Park, NJ: Hillhouse Press, 1960) p. 35.

- *Alpha Alcoholism* — psychological dependence, damaging to personal inter-relationships but exhibiting no loss of control. May develop in the wake of stresses.
- *Beta Alcoholism* — characterized by nutritional deficiency diseases, gastritis, cirrhosis of the liver, etc., but again without loss of control, withdrawal, or other addictive manifestations. Tends to occur in deprived groups—particularly those with poor nutrition.
- *Gamma alcoholism* — involves true physiological addiction, loss of control, craving, withdrawal symptoms and progressive damage in all areas of a person's life.
- *Delta alcoholism* — a need to maintain a certain minimum level of inebriation. Very difficult to detect, but causes gradual social disintegration over a period of time.
- *Epsilon Alcoholism* — periodic binges with abstinent periods between. May experience no craving or struggle to maintain sobriety, but when the binge hits, little can be done to prevent it from taking its course. It is the most puzzling type.

Jellinek, himself, recognized the complexity of the disease and felt that his typology was open to modification and that individuals could slip from one to the other type, thus confusing even these definitions. Still these five types and much of Jellinek's research are still basic knowledge today.

Yet, in the thinking and writing of most current researchers and clinicians, alcoholism is largely limited to what Jellinek described as the addictive types—Gamma, Delta and Epsilon with emphasis on the Gamma type. It is the dominant type in North America. Furthermore, AA operates on the premise that the Gamma type is alcoholism and while appropriating some characteristics of the other types (e.g., Delta and Epsilon) they feel Gamma is *it*. This has left Alpha and Beta describing conditions which are often referred to as alcohol abuse. Unfortunately, a good deal of the terminology used in lectures and writing does not reflect these changes in thinking and emphasis which have occurred over the years since Jellinek first outlined his ideas.

Another factor clouding the total picture in recent years is the emphasis growing out of the great need for research, subsequent education and treatment centering on alcoholism. What may be called alcohol abuse has been left to trail behind.

Adding still more to the confusion is that alongside the development of the concept of alcoholism as a disease, there has been an influential opinion in the psychiatric profession that insists that it is a mental health problem, i.e., a *symptom of pre-existing* psychological problems which if treated properly psychiatrically, will cause the alcoholism to disappear. Some of the proponents of this theory use the term alcohol abuse when speaking of all problems with alcohol including alcoholism.

The concept of alcoholism as a physiological disease, however, which may produce or exacerbate psychological problems has been validated by a great deal of research, which has weakened the psychiatric theory and caused many of its proponents to repudiate this stance. There are still available a great many books and articles written ten or 15 years ago based on the mental health premise.

But in this confusing forest, we need to consider some salient points. *Alcohol abuse* should more properly be called alcohol misuse. Some also identify it as problem drinking.[54] Yet, it seems that *alcohol abuse,* as a frequently used term, is a serviceable term. We can define it as:

> The inappropriate or thoughtless use by non-alcoholic persons of alcoholic beverages which can cause a multitude of problems resulting at the least in unhappiness and at the most, havoc in the life of the drinker and in the lives of others.

To illustrate, alcohol is abused when it is used:

- just before or while driving an automobile.
- just before or while piloting a boat.
- just before or while piloting a plane.
- during pregnancy.
- to unwind, relieve stress.
- on a dare — "chug-a-lugging" can be fatal.
- in hazing activities.
- to warm the body in very cold situations—pores are opened and freezing is facilitated.
- in the hot-tub—opens the pores and causes the body to become too hot.

---

[54] Alcoholism—dependence or addiction to alcohol—is problem drinking or alcohol abuse, but not all problem drinking or alcohol abuse is alcoholism. See also: James E. Royce, *Alcohol Problems and Alcoholism* (New York: The Free Press, A Division of Macmillan Publishing Co., Inc., 1981) p. 12.

- to muster courage — to seduce a woman—or a man—or to commit a crime.
- to manage grief, loneliness, boredom, guilt, depression, empty-nest syndrome.
- to manipulate others by getting them drunk.
- by violence-prone persons — may result in child or spouse abuse, incest, rape, murder.
- as the main attraction at a party or social or other event (fund raisers?).
- to celebrate, get high — drunk.
- to be one of the gang — prove one's adulthood or masculinity.

and there are many more!

We need to lessen the confusion about alcohol abuse. Frequently the newspapers or other media report some tragic "alcohol involved" event, giving few details which leaves the audience, by and large, to deduce through inference whether the involvement is alcoholism or prevalent alcohol abuse. In the case of either, average persons are unsure what to think or do, but they are ambivalent in their concern when they learn that the misuse of alcohol was involved instead of the more severe alcoholism, for "there by the grace of God, go I." As is well-known, this commonly shared feeling frequently prevents juries in rendering guilty verdicts in regard to alcohol-involved charges.

So what is the church's connection to alcohol abuse? Again, as with alcoholism, it is tied up significantly with the spiritual life and since as the church we are in the spiritual business, we must take this relationship seriously. First, we have the duty to understand and accept the Gospel message—our entry into the spiritual life which will govern our daily-living in every respect, including the use or non-use of alcohol or other drugs. Second, we are bound to share as widely as possible that message, including how it guarantees the good and full life, full of natural highs; that the especially significant experiences of life can be celebrated without the excessive use—or use, at all—of debilitating chemicals; and that the lows which inevitably come to everyone can be endured and triumphed over likewise.

Parents have an urgent responsibility at this point as they function as examples as well as teach verbally. In the congregational setting, these same truths must be shared openly and honestly in the church-school, youth groups, adult groups, with leaders and officers and also in the worship services and sermons. Recognizing the connection between our Christian convictions and our daily living is the single greatest step which can be taken to prevent the abuse-misuse of alcohol or any other drug. We do what we do because of what we *really* believe.

An additional facet of prevention is the responsibility of conscientious church members to the society in which the church exists to help establish a milieu which is conducive to lessening alcohol abuse through influencing community attitudes, customs and legislation; and to advocate proper care for those already suffering the consequences of the abusive use of alcohol.

The bottom line is that we in the church need to hear plainly and act decisively in regard to the connection between the Gospel message and how it specifically relates to the use of alcohol and other drugs. Unfortunately, as it is now, there is seldom a sermon or lesson on the subject. Who–how–when are we going to hear? Will it be through a tragic experience such as happened in my own church?

One chilly, grey, January Sunday morning, the congregation sat stunned. What exactly did the minister say? Someone was killed last night–who? Listen to the prayer, maybe you'll get the name.

Georgia Redmond! She was that lovely 18-year old with wavy, dark hair and sparkling smile who sang in the choir, was a leader in the youth group and a student body officer in her high school, too. Her style was gentle and confident–now she was gone–just like that!

As the story came out, we learned that she was on her way home a little after midnight, the passenger in her boyfriend Bill's car. Suddenly (how else!) a fast-moving automobile approaching from a side street hit their car, hurling Georgia from the car. She was dead on arrival at the hospital; Bill was critically hurt. While the ambulance attendants were putting the young people in the ambulances, the driver of the other car casually told the officers that sure, he had had a "couple of drinks" during the evening. He just hadn't seen the stop sign!

"I will never again hear the doorbell ring at night without collapsing inside," Georgia's mother told me later.

The funeral was the largest ever held in our church–young people from the high school and junior college crowded in with many other grieving friends of all ages. An undercurrent of feeling ran through the congregation.

Was it anger? confusion? despair? Would people never learn, even with all the publicity about drunk-driving?

That was four years ago. Life has gone on with many difficult days for Georgia's parents and sister who have learned consciously to live in God's strength day by day. The delays in the trial of the drinking-driver tore open the wounds again and again, but healing is at last taking place.

What of our church congregation as we lived through this experience? In the beginning the pastors and others comforted mightily. There were prayers offered; cards and notes sent; and calls of condolence made. Close friends and relatives helped in many ways, but the anger, confusion and despair continued to simmer beneath for many.

As the weeks went on, some church members thought over their personal stance vis-à-vis alcoholic beverages and decided to limit or eliminate their use. Perceiving that "it *could* happen here," many found courage to speak out about drinking and driving; the administrative body re-affirmed the rule that alcoholic beverages should not be served at church-sponsored functions, in or away from the church building. Others joined in church and community efforts to do something about careless drunk-driving. However, for many, the drinking has gone on as usual for those who want it that way.

Nevertheless, life is not the same in our congregation. When there are other deaths of young people in our largely rural county because of drunk driving—and there are one or two every month—it seems there is a return of the sadness coupled with a sensitivity that wasn't there before. We are facing up a bit, but at what a price!

The last paragraph of the theological statement of the *Report and Recommendations on the Social and Health Effects of Alcohol Use and Abuse* which was published by the 1986 General Assembly of the Presbyterian Church (U.S.A.) gives us the challenge:

> God sets before us a promise of life, of new birth and wholeness, of Shalom that needs to be proclaimed and lived out. As individuals and together as the church we can choose death or life. It is our calling to choose life and to help others to choose life, to choose Shalom.[55]

---

[55] "Shalom: The State of Whole and Ordered Righteousness," *Alcohol Use & Abuse: The Social and Health Effects* (Louisville, KY: General Assembly of the Presbyterian Church [U.S.A.]) 1986, pp. 32-34. This article was originally written by C. Howard Wallace, a professor at Dubuque Theological Seminary, Dubuque, IA.

PART III

THE CHURCH DOES ❖

8

Setting Up a Program ❖

Having recruited a task force as suggested in chapter four, one of the first steps in starting an effective alcohol ministry is to forge a program designed to meet specific local needs. Start with studying the situation in your chosen area until you reach a consensus about what you want to launch as your project. Even though this first effort may seem simple, it is important that you attack it seriously and follow through. You will gain experience and interest by doing so. Strike while the iron is hot!

There are many possible projects and programs for an initial agenda, but here are some general suggestions and comments to keep in mind while carrying out such activities.

First, early on draw up a policy statement relating to your congregation, regional group or higher administrative level—whichever is the one you propose to work through. Write down the guidelines you agree on regarding the use of alcohol and the need you recognize in regard to alcohol problems along with what you perceive can reasonably be done in ministry concerning them.

Make this a simple and short statement. Refer to the pronouncements of your particular denomination on this issue and if possible look at those produced by other denominations. Brainstorm about the expressed views and then write your own statement which will meet your specific needs and concerns, adapting it as necessary. This exhilarating experience will not only give you a base to work from, but will allow the task force to own your policy statement and give you a base to work from.

Practical expediency will probably require you to present your guidelines to the governing body of the entity in which you intend to work, seeking their concurrence. This, in itself, will provide an educational opportunity!

Second, it is vital that the clergy take an active pastoral role, even though lay persons may have initiated the ministry because for ministry of this nature to succeed in the congregation, it is imperative the pastoral team be supportive, and because this is a true mission field of the congregation. In my experience, not all pastors are eager to get involved in such ministry and some have been notably reluctant to do anything about alcohol problems in their congregations.

This seems incredible in view of the finding that more alcoholics continue to have initial contact concerning their drinking problems with clergy than all other professional persons combined.[50] Beyond this, there are the countless family members who go to their pastors in search of help with their domestic problems which are caused or aggravated by alcohol. Truly the church cannot miss this opportunity to reach out with Christian compassion to draw hurting and seeking people into the circle of God's love.

It appears that many clerics are reluctant to get involved in this needy but fruitful ministry because of little information or training being given in their seminaries or training institutes in dealing with alcohol problems. Having little knowledge these clergy are insecure about dealing with alcohol abuse and with their busy schedules find it easy to push such a ministry into the background. This is doubly regrettable since alcoholism and alcohol abuse have a definite spiritual basis which should be included in pastoral theology courses—regardless of time constraints and curriculum concerns. (See Appendix IV for a list of seminaries which offer courses in this area.)

Few there are who have been in the pastorate for even a few years who have not run into alcohol problems, knowingly or not. Thus any hesitation to seek or accept professional training remains incomprehensible. Rev.

[56] Paul C. Conley and Andrew A. Sorensen, *The Staggering Steeple* (Philadelphia: United Church Press, 1971) p. 127.

Karl A. Schneider, a Lutheran who was director for several years of the outstanding Eagleville Hospital and Rehabilitation Center in Pennsylvania, lists ten "stumbling blocks" which he says inhibit clergy from seeking training in dealing with alcohol problems. In summary they are:

1. *The good-guy syndrome* — afraid to risk offending church members by identifying or dealing with their alcohol problems.
2. *The "perfect" pastors* — who cannot admit such problems exist in their perfect (?) congregations.
3. *Personal drinking patterns* — might make taking a look at them a risky business!
4. *"Let George do it"* — let someone else, some other pastor or some other agency take care of these problems.
5. *"I haven't encountered an alcoholism situation in years"* — of course, there having been no demonstrated caring in this regard, no one comes to the pastor with such a problem.
6. *Fear of failure* — perhaps based on previous painful attempts to deal with alcohol problems.
7. *Frustration* — a falsely perceived lack of general success in treatment of alcoholism.
8. *"It's a moral problem"* — lack of understanding of alcoholism as a physical disease with spiritual dimensions.
9. *"What about youth-drinking?"* — serves as a smoke screen to avoid looking at adult alcohol abuse.
10. *Personal need to be a "rescuer"* — "fixing" becomes enabling so efforts fail for the alcoholic, the family and the pastor.

Schneider's concluding premise is that when pastors deal realistically with these stumbling blocks, they turn into stepping-stones to a valuable ministry with alcohol problems.[57]

Recently I sat up till dawn reading Suzanne Somer's story of her growing-up in a tumultuous and miserable home because of her father's alcoholism. Her mother, a devout Catholic who attended Mass every morning, managed to survive by sheer force by making a life for herself, mostly in her parish church.

Suzanne's recollection is that there was no help in the church for their domestic problems for, as she says, "The Catholic Church provided only spiritual guidance. No one in the clergy was trained in substance-abuse and dealing with family co-addicts."[58] Neither did any of the nuns in the parochial schools which she and her siblings attended tumble to the reason for the continually uncompleted homework or habitual falling asleep in class. Instead, they were labelled "dumb." After 30 incredible years of misery, all the members of her family, including her father, discovered AA, Al-Anon and treatment which led to recovery. Today Suzanne is the honorary chairperson of the National Association for Children of Alcoholics in which she is very active.

This story is by no means a reflection on the Catholic

[57] Karl L. Schneider, *Stumbling Blocks or Stepping Stones: Overcoming Inhibiting Attitudes to Involvement in Early Intervention and Training in Alcohol and Drug Problems* (New York: National Council on Alcoholism, 1982) pp. 3-8.
[58] Suzanne Somers, *Keeping Secrets* (New York: Warner Books, Inc., 1988) p. 40.

Church in particular, for all churches are equally culpable. And even though the overall situation in the churches and among pastors has improved somewhat in recent years, there is still a very long way to go.

Yet Suzanne's story suggests another question: Are we letting other groups take the lead in this ministry, even though we in the church hold the basic answer to these problems? The church must not forget these hurting families in our midst whose difficulties could be alleviated.

Third, Scripture teaches us that the laity of the church are strengthened and guided by the Holy Spirit to exercise special gifts of ministry (see 1 Co 12:4-11). These gifts are crucial to the welfare of the church community. Thus we can expect to find a church community with individuals who have particular interests, education and vocations who are valuable in this wholistic ministry faced by the church. It is imperative that the church use them all.

Fourth, establishing a specific alcohol ministry may be arduous going at first—despite there being many who are needing such help. The best advice for a new committee is to build a supportive constituency of interested persons within the larger group in which you want to function. This might mean working person to person with little fanfare, contacting pastors by letter and telephone follow-up, asking for support at board and organization meetings while presenting concerns and proposals. Offering to present a series of educational classes for youth or adults is a good place to start, because information engenders interest. Such a series can "travel" to nearby churches and district meetings also. Building on interest generated from such programs might mean being included in worship services, or leafletting the congregation with appropriate literature. Interested people will be identified and can be drawn in to enlarge the task force.

Fifth, beyond working in your local congregation, it is important to reach out to other groups in your area, especially with those in which you are involved in your daily life. (There are many ideas for this reaching-out in the next chapter where suggested activities and programs are listed.)

Sixth, as you prepare to initiate a concrete program of ministry, your first step is to make a precise survey of your church congregation and of your community to determine the level of interest and activity. A lot of information can be obtained by telephone, but try to meet in person with at least one individual or group in every category listed below. Unfortunately, sending out questionnaires by mail often brings few replies and the valuable personal contact is missed as well. If you do send a letter, follow it up with a personal contact. As you solicit information, try to find out:

1. What the *general level of knowledge and interest* in alcohol problems is in your congregation and your civic entities. A simple questionnaire used in personal interviews can produce this information.
2. What the *statistical picture* is. Your city or county health departments or your law enforcement agencies should be able to help with this.
3. How do *religious and community leaders* (pastors,

counsellors, hospitals, physicians, attorneys, school personnel, business people) evaluate the local situation and how prevalent do they see alcohol problems to be and how do they rate efforts being made to deal with these?

4. What is being done within your church or community regarding *alcohol education.* Do not settle for exhibits of curricula or plans—find out what is actually being accomplished.

5. What *treatment services* exist in the community. City or county health departments should be able to help you with names and locations. The *Yellow Pages* tend to be a good source, but visit as many of these locations as feasible, finding out their basic philosophy of treatment, the training and experience of their personnel, who is eligible for treatment, the size of operation, the cost and requirements for insurance eligibility and then, importantly, their perceived success rate. Observation of the facilities as to cleanliness, furnishings and attractiveness is also important.

This is no small task, depending on how thoroughly you go into detail. Try not to get in too deeply, but remember that everything you learn will be invaluable as you set about establishing your own program. The data assembled will furnish a lot of information, hence ammunition, to use as you seek to educate others and implement programs in your church and community. It will also furnish a basis for filling out forms for grants, if you decide to apply for such help.

As you evaluate your findings, aim to draw up a realistic picture of the needs and the current efforts to meet them. Then determine where you might best put your energies.

Reflect on the needs you have discovered vis-à-vis the lists of ideas and resources in the next chapter. Use your imagination and ingenuity in adapting these suggestions to your needs—or to the development of new types of programs. Like the Biblical mustard seed, let your ideas grow and carry on—as someone has said—with bold Christian concern!

9

Programs in Progress – and Ideas for More ❖

There are myriad suggestions compiled in these lists, but this in no ways implies that anyone should take a "the more the merrier" approach. Rather they are all included to help you see the possibilities for ministry in diverse situations.

The listings are arranged under the headings:

1. Ministry by an individual – lay or clergy.
2. Ministry in and through a congregation.
3. Ministry through regional entities or coalitions.
4. Ministry though upper levels of church denominations.

You will discover there is some overlapping among

the lists, but this merely reflects the fact that some ministries can be carried on by one or many persons in varying situations.

A large number of the programs listed are in progress at the present time and others are suggested as ways to meet perceived needs. Many of the ideas have come through the invaluable information sent me while I was editor of the newsletter of the *Presbyterian Network on Alcohol and Other Drug Abuse* (PNAODA). Credit for their contributions are referenced (by § number) in Appendix II (see p. 192). Other ideas I have gleaned from numerous contacts with persons working in the fields.

1. Ministry by an Individual — Lay or Clergy

Are you a lone committee of one or would you like to do ministry beyond the task force of which you may be a member? Here are almost three dozen ideas which can be carried out within or outside the church on an individual basis:

1. Learn all you can about alcohol problems and how they can be dealt with. (See Appendix I, A Syllabus) [§26]
2. Visit AA, Al-Anon, Alateen, Adult Children of Alcoholics and similar groups. (If you are not a member attend the open meetings.) [§58]
3. Share your knowledge and concerns informally with others and more formally as a speaker at church groups, service clubs, school classes, student clubs, parents' school associations. [§6, 35, 59]
4. If you are a recovering alcoholic or family-member,

share your recovery experience and knowledge in the same ways as suggested in number three.

5. If there is no AA, Al-Anon, Alateen or Adult Children's group in your neighborhood, town or workplace, try to get one going. Offer the church for a meeting place. (See also about eleventh-step groups under suggestions for the congregation.) [29, 35, 43, 51]

6. Offer to be a liaison / contact person in your church to help in these ways: [16, 65]

   • Learn about services in your community and assist those seeking help to find the help they need. [55, 85]

   • share books and pamphlets with those who have problems or those who want to learn more about alcohol problems. Place pamphlets in the church literature rack. [57]

   • be a friend to recovering alcoholics and their families. Invite them to your church worship, to participate in social activities, and to your home when feasible. [100, 102]

This story came to me in a letter from the recent widow of a rural pastor about what she calls "high-risk undertakings" in one-to-one ministry. She writes:

David came to the church, seeking help. He spent a month in de-tox and rehab at the state hospital. After a few unsuccessful attempts at sobriety, and a few different jobs on some area ranches, David ended up in jail for driving under the influence. . . . My husband decided that what David needed was food on a regular basis and some "family," so that spring and summer David ate his lunch and supper with our family, which included five children, and we insisted that he "relax" in our TV and family room for the evening. He was to be my "handy-man." . . . He helped the children with all the regular household chores each evening. . . . By fall we had found a janitorial job for him. However, at our invitation (and mild persuasion) he continued eating with our family and spending the evening at our house. During this time he attended church regularly (sitting in the back row in silence). . . . My husband liked to get him into friendly arguments about football . . . and these arguments even became a means whereby he started coming out of his shell. Now, eleven years of sobriety behind him, he is head custodian of a Middle School; . . . he is unofficially in charge of lights, heat and ushering at the church. He moved into a small home of his own after having "shared" our family life for over two years. He has at various times loaned our kids money for college, "supervised" the house and the teenagers living there while my husband and I were on vacations and is fondly thought of as "Uncle Dave".

She adds that at one time her husband's brother who is a recovering alcoholic lived with them for two years and eventually moved into his own home, has a job and continues in sobriety. Finally she says:

This type of ministry to alcoholics takes lots of adjustment and commitment . . . and faith . . . but it has worked for the above two individuals. Thanks be to God! §102

(This friend signed her name, but she wishes to remain

anonymous and says that "Uncle Dave" is not his real name.)

- Help individuals and families to make necessary arrangements such as financial help, child-care, job-saving, when treatment is necessary. §17, 56, 77
- Visit, if possible, those in recovery facilities; send them get-well or thinking-of-you cards. §37
- Be a special friend to families shattered because of tragic drunken behavior—their own or others.

7. Share your knowledge and interest on your job with co-workers including supervisors or bosses. §89

8. Volunteer to help in church and community alcohol programs; serve on councils, committees and boards of directors. §4, 12, 33, 52, 72, 82, 95

9. Support church and community programs financially and with in-kind contributions.

10. Join and support organizations such as *Mothers Against Drunk-Driving* (MADD), the local office of the *National Council on Alcoholism* (NCA), *National Federation of Parents for Drug Free Youth,* and others of national scope.

11. Find out about, support and join your denominational or regional group which works on ministry regarding alcohol problems, §7 and health. §33, 76

12. Become a qualified alcohol counselor—a second career, perhaps! §12, 44, 49, 58, 62, 92, 93

13. If you are a professional person, incorporate knowledge of alcohol problems into your practice. §32, 87

14. If you are a school teacher, counsellor, administrator, incorporate your knowledge and interest into your daily work with your students. §50

15. If you are not a professional person, try to raise

awareness among the professional people you contact, e.g., doctor, dentist, lawyer, your child's school teacher or principal.

16. Become a court counsellor, working with the probation department.

17. Teach DUI (driving under the influence) classes in conjunction with the courts. $§42$

18. Support good legislation, enlisting others to do so, too. Join your state's *Council on Alcohol Problems.* $§63, 96$

19. Write letters or articles for the local newspaper and church magazines. Write your own story! $§34, 54, 84$

20. Write a regular column for your church newsletter. $§71$

21. Make up a directory of local services.

22. Work on Skid Row, through missions, soup-kitchens, ministry to the homeless and police programs. $§73$

23. Encourage and enlist others to become involved in "doing something" about alcohol problems through the church. Start a movement! $§55, 75, 79$

The following suggestions are particularly for pastors:

24. Lead your church governing board in discussion of the use of alcoholic beverages at church functions, including wine in the observance of the Lord's Supper. $§28, 91$

25. Occasionally attend AA and related groups which meet in your church. Offer to give devotions and invite them to church services and functions. (Inquire ahead of time about attending regular meetings.) $§7, 90$

26. Offer to hear "5th Steps" of AA. $§8, 47, 85, 90$

27. Offer to conduct informal worship or other pastoral services in treatment centers. $§21, 36, 69$

28. Devote an occasional Sunday worship service to the subject of alcohol problems, having testimonies from

recovering persons. §40

29. Preach sermons about the use and non-use of alcoholic beverages and lead discussions on your points among the church membership. §19

30. Include these various aspects routinely in public and private prayer.

31. Relate the spiritual aspects of alcohol use to evangelism. §37

32. Include discussion about the use of alcohol and other drugs in confirmation classes, marriage counselling—particularly previous to the wedding—and in new member preparation.

33. Raise your concerns in your local ministerial association, and at your denominational regional level. §66

34. Convene a prayer and Bible-study group for recovering alcoholics and family members of alcoholics. §57, 60, 87, 102

35. If you are a chaplain in a hospital, other institution, or in the military, be knowledgeable about alcohol problems and aggressive in working for solutions.

2. Ministry in and through a Congregation

These are suggestions for ministry within and through a local congregation. They assume that a committee or task force exists which has studied about alcoholism and other alcohol abuse and which is knowledgeable about their congregation's needs and possibilities in regard to alcohol ministry. It is also assumed that additional persons will be drawn in to carry out projects of the ministry—the original committee doesn't need to do it all!

1. *Establish a consistent program of education.*

   Education about alcohol use—or non-use—when done properly, can well be the most effective contribution the church can make in prevention of alcohol problems both within its own bounds and the larger community because the church deals with fundamental concepts for living—why we do what we do, and should do, to live successfully with ourselves, others and before God. Additionally, the church is in a unique position to carry on a program of information and motivation because of its organizational set-up, consisting of classes or groups of all ages, dedicated teachers and leaders and basic curricula. §100

   - Begin by drawing up a plan of education for the whole congregation to be implemented cyclically over a period of one to three years. Break it down into manageable units as to subjects, groups, and leadership. §8, 86 (There are several curricula outlines listed in Appendix IV, and your denomination may have courses available.) Schedule enough classes or events in number and of sufficient length so that there is time for worthwhile presentations of the subject matter followed by opportunity for questions and discussion. Be prepared for persons who speak to the leader personally about problems—their own or in their families. This is a real opportunity for vital ministry.

   - Include classes for these persons or groups as you plan:
     - Pastors (if not already a part of your committee) and the official boards of your church. §42
     - Lay-employees—they are often the first ones approached by persons seeking help.

- Sunday church school teachers—all ages.
- Week-day groups, e.g., children's clubs, choirs, family-nights, Bible and issue studies, released time. §27
- Fellowship and service organizations—e.g., women's, men's, youth, couples, singles, senior citizen clubs. §64
- Summer camps and retreats.
- Worship services (Alcohol Awareness Sunday, etc.) §44

• Cover these subjects:
- General information about alcohol, alcohol abuse, alcoholism, personal choice, stigma, denial.
- Biblical, spiritual and theological aspects.
- Your denominational and local church stance.
- What can be done for those already suffering from alcohol abuse or alcoholism.
- Prevention of problems including changing societal attitudes and importance of legislation. §90
- Social skills, especially for youth and young adults, which enable one to feel at ease without alcohol.

• Methods:
- Include in regular curricula of church school and youth groups.
- Programs with speakers, videos, films, discussions and workshops.
- Visits to AA, Al-Anon, Alateen, Adult Children groups and study of their literature. §37
- Peer-counsellor training, especially for youth. §9
- Church newsletter articles. §71
- Inserts in Sunday worship bulletins.

— "Minutes for mission." §14
— Pamphlets — handed out and also placed in narthex literature rack.
— Books in the church library. §57
— Sermons and testimonies. §19, 40
— Discussion of commercial movies dealing with drinking.
— Send leaders to training courses and workshops.
— Tour treatment facilities and programs nearby.
— Promote Alcohol Awareness weeks sponsored by state or national organization.§44

2. *Develop programs in the church to meet the needs of persons in the congregation and those from the community who may come to the church for help.* Education alone will not do the job, there must be action, too!

   • Assemble a nucleus helping team of knowledgeable people who will help individuals and families in solving drinking problems. Included as far as possible should be a pastor or other spiritual leader, a recovering alcoholic, a physician, a lawyer, a social worker and a financial advisor. This team will assist persons in finding treatment including AA or related groups: in getting an alcoholic into treatment; in finding child-care, housing, employment, legal or financial assistance, when necessary, and looking out for follow-up needs. §17

   • If possible, appoint an alcohol program coordinator or liaison person who will oversee the ministry in and through the congregation. This could well be a qualified recovering alcoholic, or a family member of a recovering person. If the church is large, this could even be a paid staff person, or if it is of lesser size, this could be a dedicated volunteer. In any event, this person should have some training in dealing with alcohol problems. The nucleus helping team will then function as a valuable resource. (A list of suggested activities for a liaison person appears under #6, in the section devoted to ministry as an individual.) The size of such a ministry will depend a great deal on the location of your church—inner-city, suburban, rural, etc.—and on the cultural, ethnic and age milieu of your congregation and community.

- As a committee and a congregation invite AA and related groups to meet in the church facilities.$^{§29, 68}$ Invite them to attend services (but do not make this a requirement for using your building). Take pains to invite them to come to special celebrations such as Christmas, New Year's or other festive days when loneliness can take over. $^{§7, 90}$

- Schedule Bible studies and prayer groups for recovering persons, family members and concerned friends.

- Organize groups which emphasize Christ as the "higher power," e.g., weekly brown-bag lunches,^{§25} Vineyard Ministry,^{§18} Alcoholics Victorious, Overcomers, Taste of New Wine,^{§47} Seekers.^{§46} These might all be called "eleventh-step" groups.$^{§2, 23, 34, 61}$

- Establish a financial assistance fund and child-care help for persons in recovery centers.$^{§56, 77}$

- Review the membership of your church to see if any might be "falling through the cracks." Consult the categories listed in the next section to see who these people might be and what might be done.

3. *Reaching into your community, develop or cooperate in existing programs which promote awareness, prevention and treatment of alcohol problems.*

- Develop programs for special populations, some of whom may be in your congregation or on the fringes, but others are out in the community. Using church facilities for friendship, recreational, educational or problem-solving groups may well provide viable prevention of alcohol problems as well as opportunity to identify already existing problems. Personal calling in the homes is also a good method of accomplishing the same goals and often will uncover other needs.

  Some of these special populations are:

- Ethnic or language groups — refugees or new immigrants who may not understand the responsible use of alcoholic beverages in American society and also groups who, though long-time residents, have special difficulties, e.g., Native Americans.

- Disabled persons — often ignored in this respect but frequently vulnerable to alcohol abuse.

- Elderly persons — those living alone or in retirement complexes often suffer boredom, depression and despair which leads to excessive drinking.

- Homeless — many of the people surviving on the streets today are not the usual wanderers, but simply cannot find or afford a home. Drink becomes a solace, then a problem in such a situation.

- Women — who are often overlooked in dealing with alcohol problems—either their own alcoholism or as a co-dependent. Family problems, depression, divorce, children's problems etc., are often the indicators of alcohol abuse. Alcoholism combined with other drug abuse is very often both the cause and effect of women in prostitution.

- Military personnel from nearby military bases ^{§81} and veterans seeking help with drug and alcohol problems.
- Youth — who frequently say "there's nothing to do in this town!" Some suggestions in reply:

  — a street ministry especially on "cruising nights" when beer consumption and drug dealing are rife.

  — recreation: dances, proms, graduation parties, athletics, a night club—all without alcohol.

  — sponsor an essay or poster contest with worthwhile prizes.

  — have youth present plays and other entertainment about alcohol use to youth and children in the schools and community events. ^{§47}
- Skid-row (road) — for inner-city churches this is a real challenge. In regard to these particular alcohol problems, law enforcement and other city or county programs leave much to be desired—often because of financial limitations. As a non-governmental entity, the church is often able to provide what is missing. To develop a sensible, realistic, healing, non-patronizing program, study and consultation with other agencies and individuals engaged in the work must be undertaken. (See Books in Appendix IV for two realistic books.)
- Jails and prisons — contact the jail or prison chaplain to find out what is already being done. If there is no AA group, work to get one started. Suggest screening to identify alcoholics and others with alcohol problems. Join in visitation of prisoners under the auspices of a reliable organization,

(Charles Colson's Prison Fellowship, e.g.) In addition, a friendship group in the church to befriend newly released prisoners would be a great boon. §13 A concerned state prison chaplain reports that this is a real need because often the newly released prisoner has no one on the outside to be friends with, so the temptation is to go back to the familiar bar or tavern to find companionship which frequently lands them back in prison. All facets of this ministry take very dedicated special people, but it does make a dent in the system. Women in prison also must be remembered. §24, 32

- Workers who have been laid off when the plant closes and farmers who have been foreclosed on often over-drink in their despair and idleness.
- Gays and lesbians — the rate of alcoholism in homosexual communities is one in four, compared to one in ten in the general population. Gay AA groups exist in the larger cities but more are needed there and in smaller communities.

4. *Establish treatment facilities for alcoholics and/or shelters for families affected by them.*
   - A social-model recovery home §1, 52 for alcoholics— men or women, or geared to a specific group, e.g., impaired professional persons, §30, 32 Native-Americans, African-Americans, §98 Hispanics, gays and lesbians, youth, elderly, disabled, etc.

In my experience, the social-model recovery homes for alcoholics and other drug abusers has proven more effective as compared to the medical model which is programs are good, they tend to be expensive, thus excluding those who do not have insurance coverage. The length of treatment in such facilities usually varies from ten to 28 days with some follow-up.

On the other hand, social-model recovery programs offer treatment regimens in a home-like atmosphere that last from 90 days to six months. This enables a good start on a new life-style. They are much less expensive, often geared to the financial means of the person in treatment. Frequently the local city or county will provide general relief assistance for destitute persons, and many insurance policies will now cover the expense. Medical back-up is usually required.

The fact that they are often supported, at least in part, by local contributions gives the community a basic interest. They lend themselves naturally to church sponsorship and support. The social-model is readily adaptable to other types of homes and shelters also.

Setting up a recovery home or other shelter is quite an undertaking. The most essential element in such a project is a dedicated and enthusiastic cadre of persons to spearhead and continue working on the project. This team should visit similar nearby treatment centers to gather information on as many aspects of operation as possible to learn what the possibilities are. Another crucial element is a reliable source of financial support both for the setting-up and operating expenses. Fees alone will not support such a program.

Unless a single congregation is large and well endowed, it may be wise to enlist a consortium of churches to work on such a project. Service clubs, health and law-enforcement entities and other community organizations may be interested in working on such a project as well. Some government money (federal and state) is possibly available, but such grants entail much paper-work and tantalizing uncertainty. The freedom and local control which comes with entirely voluntary support and fees—although sometimes shaky—must be weighed against larger government sums with their built-in problems. (An excellent book on this subject is listed under Books in Appendix IV: *Social Model Alcohol Recovery*).

As mentioned earlier, establishing a recovery home for alcoholics was what spurred me into dealing with alcohol problems. This has proved to be a grand adventure and I thank God for it and the hundreds of men and women who have found new lives in sobriety because of the projects I have been involved with.

Other needed treatment and shelter facilities:
- An after-treatment living facility for recovering alcoholics. This is crucial because there is both the need to build new friendships and also help the recovering person during this period of lessened income. §85, 94, 100
- A shelter for spouses and children who have been abused physically, mentally or emotionally by an alcoholic family member. §78
- A long-term live-in facility for teenagers afflicted with alcoholism and other drug abuse, but who have poor family support. This might be run in cooperation with the probation department which will pay for assignees.
- A child-care facility for children of alcoholics in treatment or while attending AA meetings. The former may have to be a boarding home. Care for their children is

a major stumbling block to women needing to go into treatment.

- An outpatient program for treating and stabilizing youth or adults who have alcohol or drug problems. One of the most successful ventures with which I have been involved is such a service. A small group from eight churches stepped out on faith in the 1960s to hire a young man to direct a program which would deal with high-school students. It now has centers in several cities and towns, supported by churches, individuals and government grants. However, most important is that thousands of young people have recovered from their addictions. (See Turning-Point in list of programs in Appendix IV.)

5. *Support and assist established recovery centers or outpatient programs which depend on community support,* by: §68
   - Financial and in-kind gifts.
   - Soliciting donations during fund drives.
   - Volunteering to teach crafts, tutor, lead sings, coach sports.
   - Doing or supervising handy-person tasks.
   - Helping in regard to alcohol problems in neighborhood type community programs.
   - Offering alcohol-problem awareness training for staff in shelters, thrift shops, soup kitchens, etc.
   - Offering to help on telephone "help-lines" which deal with alcohol problems particularly.
   - Serving on advisory committees or planning boards.
   - Soliciting other churches or organizations for support for these centers or programs.

6. *And* —
   - Present workshops and conferences for interested groups or work with other sponsoring groups. §48 *Note:* There seems to be a blind spot in the minds of many professional workshop or conference planners in regard to including ministry in the church subjects in their programs and having knowledgeable church leaders taking part; and likewise, it seems interested church people do not notice that they are left out or that they should ask to be included. The planners' position is possibly due to a largely erroneous feeling that churches in general are not interested, or that they may be too negative and uninformed in their thinking to be helpful. There may be some basis for these feelings, but given that the solution to alcohol problems is spiritual,[59] subjects and leaders relating to church ministry should be included in workshops and conferences. Knowledgeable church persons can correct this matter by being alert and asking to be included.
   - Cooperate in community or school "No-To-Alcohol" weeks.
   - Organize a "First-Nighter" program for the town's New Year's Eve celebration. §53
   - Write articles and letters to the local newspaper; get them to do an investigative series; submit

---

[59] As noted earlier, there are discussions and books on spirituality, but these are often vague when it comes to definition and explanation. Persons more definitely in the spiritual business, such as pastors and Christian leaders, could well make valuable contributions here in workshops and conferences.

recipes for non-alcoholic drinks for the food pages.
- Publicize and support good legislation concerning alcoholic beverages at all government levels.
- Cooperate with community organizations doing prevention programs, e.g., Parent Teachers Association, Parents For Drug-Free Youth, Jay-cees.
- Compile and circulate a directory of alcoholism services in the community.
- Whatever your project, keep your congregation regularly informed and invite their participation.

3. Ministry through Denominational Regional Entities or Coalitions of Churches

The lists in this section are for the district or intermediate organizational levels of a denomination. The suggestions are also adaptable to a group of churches within a geographical area uniting together ^{§59} and to women's, men's or youth organizations of the regional entities. ^{§67} Because of the scope of these ideas, they are better carried out by a larger group than a local congregation.

Ministry in regard to alcohol problems at the district level probably falls under the heading of social concerns in the organizational structure. Sometimes a sub-committee on alcohol ministry, tied into the social concerns (or whatever it may be called) committee works well. This arrangement allows additional persons with a special interest in this ministry to join in with the one or two social concerns committee members who have been appointed to care for this aspect of social ministry. On the other hand, a district organization—seeing the importance of alcohol ministry—may determine that a group concerned with it should be a full-fledged committee within its jurisdiction. $\S 3, 15, 74, 78$

This committee, sub- or free-standing, may already be in existence, but in need of new life, or it may be the outgrowth of a nucleus of persons who have been studying and working to raise consciousness at the district level, and having had a modicum of success are invited to become a part of the total social concerns ministry. Of course, it might be a group of newly appointed persons charged to study the matter, promote awareness and go into action. In any event, following is a list of projects or programs which are particularly adapted to being carried out at the district level by a dedicated committee.

1. *Raise awareness of pastors and other church leaders by:*
   - Person to person conversation, i.e., pastors to pastors, leaders to leaders. $\S 45$
   - Committee contacts with key individuals or governing boards.
   - Giving out pamphlets, and circulating books and cassettes.
   - Presenting informational speakers at the regular plenary meetings of the district, e.g., pastors who are working in the alcoholism field; prevention and treatment therapists; representatives of organizations which work on legislation or education. $\S 36$
   - Presenting a worship service at plenary meetings.$\S 3$
   - Giving out information on pertinent public policy matters.

2. *Provide training for clergy and lay-persons through:*
   - Presenting workshops, free-standing or included in periodic district events such as summer camps and conferences (youth and adult); training sessions for officers, church-school teachers, youth leaders, church office personnel; even mission rallies. §85 Insist on a good time "slot" at these events—not opposite the featured speaker of the day! Also, beware of ending up with a remote, dark corner for your meeting place. Your subject needs every advantage you can get and is important! §15, 62
   - Compiling a manual of information, programs and resources for leaders at the local or regional level to use. §80
   - Arranging an on-going, week-long, live-in training program for pastors with a local recovery center and providing scholarships for them to attend. §22
   - Acquainting pastors and lay-persons with two- or three-day educational opportunities offered by training institutes and universities and, again, provide scholarships for them to attend.
   - Providing peer-counselling training for youth. §9
   - Providing alcohol ministry training for candidates for ordination if they have not had it already in seminary.
   - Making educational and program materials—videos, films, tapes, books, curricula—available on a loan basis for member churches and groups.

3. *Sponsor programs which are more easily done on a regional basis,* e.g.:
   - Assemble a nucleus helping-team of knowledgeable people on a regional basis—especially if the region

is far-flung with smaller towns. (See specifics of such a team under congregational suggestions.)

- Establish an Employees Assistance Program (EAP) for pastors and other church staff. (See the next section on suggestions for the national or central denominational level.) §88, 93

- Compile and distribute a directory of alcohol services available in the regional area.

- Sponsor outstanding speakers of national or celebrity status for the general public of the area.

- Organize retreats for recovering alcoholics and family members, drawing both from the churches and the communities.

- Establish an AA group for recovering pastors of the area, and Al-Anon for their family members. §5

- Establish and operate an alcoholism treatment facility. (See suggestions for congregations for details.) §1, 83

- Offer education and counselling in church-related retirement homes and communities, and possibly in non-church related homes.

- Work with chaplains of denominational colleges located within the regional area in promulgating information and building awareness among students and faculty. §31

- Join and support inter-denominational organizations which work on public policy and preventive education.

- Show interest and work with other groups presenting training opportunities in your area. (See congregational suggestions.)

4. Ministry through Upper Levels of Church Denominations

Many, if not most church denominations in our country are more or less held together and directed from a national or central level. Although the members in the pews are frequently not very conscious of this direction on a day-to-day basis, a church—both locally and regionally—is influenced by the decisions made at the national or central level. (Of course, it is notable how dramatically consciousness rises when an unpopular stance is taken at that level!)

In my experience, when significant concerns coincide at both the higher level and the local level they validate each other. Therefore, in regard to ministry with alcohol problems it is necessary for the highest jurisdictional level of a denomination to declare such a ministry to be important and then proceed to promote it diligently throughout its constituency. The interest may actually have begun in a local congregation or lower regional level, but it gains strength by being recognized as important higher-up; likewise, if the interest has begun at the upper level it gains validation as it meets needs, is promoted and carried out at the lower levels. Hence the importance of the programs and project suggestions in this section.

1. From the national or central level there usually are published some basic matters of doctrine, practice and church government which are for the guidance of the membership. *Among these statements should be one*

which outlines the particular denomination's stance in regard to the use or non-use of alcoholic beverages, and which expresses concern for carrying-out appropriate ministry in regard to alcoholism and other alcohol abuse. If there is not such a policy statement, or it is out of date, it might be a timely first task for a group concerned with alcohol ministry—with contacts at this level—to arouse awareness of the importance of such a statement, and also, to assist in drawing it up. Publication and circulation in an "up-front" manner of such a statement together with suggestions for carrying out its concerns will encourage alcohol ministry at all levels.

2. In most denominations of any size, certain church-wide programs are commonly administered from the national or central level. Among these are:
    - Training of the clergy (seminaries).
    - Overseas missions and some home missions.
    - Publishing of educational curricula.
    - Publication of a church-wide magazine or newspaper.
    - Publication of youth, women's and men's program guides.
    - Administration of a pension and health insurance plan for clergy.

    Particularly in these functions it is important that there be an awareness, knowledge and desire to implement ministry in regard to alcohol use and abuse in and through the church. Following are suggestions to help bring this about:

- Establish a department or office in the central headquarters which is staffed by persons who are charged with seeing that education for alcohol ministry and its implementation is included in programs administered from that level.
- Require pastoral training in dealing with alcohol problems in the seminary curriculum. $^{10, 20}$ Mary Ellen Pinkham, a sincere Christian, in her book about her own search for sobriety, says:

Unfortunately, like many other professionals, clergy . . . often don't have the slightest idea of how to help the families and friends of an alcoholic. . . . Most [clergy] are uncomfortable with the idea of alcoholism. . . . Instead of beating around the bush or playing God, the minister should be up-front and direct them [families] to Al-Anon . . . families would get help so much sooner.[60]

This also applies to dealing with alcoholics!

- Include similar training in the orientation of missionaries and overseas personnel. Alcohol problems, including alcoholism, are rife in almost all countries, both among nationals and expatriates.

Following are excerpts from letters received from missionaries while I edited the newsletter of the *Presbyterian Network on Alcohol and Other Drug Abuse:*

---

[60] Mary Ellen Pinkham, *How to Stop the One You Love From Drinking* (New York, NY, G. P. Putnam's Sons, 1986) pp. 110-111.

From Africa — Drinking has been a serious problem in Nigeria for generations. Mary Slessor was tackling the gin problem back in 1846!

From India — There are about 100 AA groups throughout India. The Catholics are doing most of these ... the Protestant Church does almost nil about the problem of alcohol. . . . Drinking is a major problem among Christians.

From Costa Rica — In this tiny country of two million people, it is estimated that one out of every seven persons . . . is affected, directly or indirectly . . . but the remedial work now going on is somewhat commensurate. There are 468 groups of AA, extending into practically every village. (This spread of AA has been largely due to one missionary, a recovering alcoholic himself, and his wife, as he taught in a seminary in San Jose.)

From Chile — A survey in Quilpue, 80 miles northwest of the capital showed 1.5 per cent of the town's children are alcoholics and 10 per cent are "excessive drinkers."

From Thailand — Alcoholism is rife here. My adopted Thai children had alcoholic parents who abandoned them. There are no laws regulating sales or consumption of alcoholic beverages here.[61]

- Such training should be provided for those working in the home field where many of the problems are alcohol related.
- It should go without saying that specific training in recognizing and dealing with alcohol problems should be required of those engaged in medical

---

[61] Personal correspondence.

missions at home or abroad.

- Include lessons and activities in the basic (not elective) curricula for church school, youth programs, and adult studies. Provide training for teachers and leaders to teach the lessons to make them effective.
- Frequently include articles promoting alcohol education and dealing with alcohol problems in the denominational magazines.
- Include coverage for alcoholism and other drug treatment in the health insurance plan of clergy and other covered personnel. §88
- Establish a church-wide employees assistance program (EAP) for all personnel, clergy or lay.

3. *Here are some additional ideas which particularly lend themselves to carrying out at or from the national or central level:*

- Work out models of ministry which are adaptable to all levels of the church, and publish and demonstrate them.
- Have a literature and publicity booth at the regular national gathering of the denomination. Provide comfortable chairs for consultation and, if feasible, take names to build a constituency.
- Present workshops and other informational events at the national meetings.
- Include alcohol concerns in the programs of women's, men's and youth periodic national meetings.
- Relate alcohol problems—their cause, effects and amelioration—to other denominational concerns often not thought of in this respect, e.g., hunger, home-

lessness, poverty, criminal justice, peacemaking, and evangelism.

- Organize interested persons throughout the denomination into an active group to advocate, advise and carry out programs.
- Let the public know through the media the church's stance and ministry in regard to alcohol problems.
- Support constructive legislation at the national level of government regarding alcohol education, sales, taxes, and funding for prevention and treatment.
- Join in ecumenical movements which promote ministry in regard to alcohol problems. [§100]
- Through the denominational publishing house, publish brochures, booklets and books for education of the membership and others in the use and abuse of alcohol.

Epilogue ❖

SO . . .

This book ends where it began: The church *should* and *can* do something about alcohol abuse and alcoholism. It is my earnest prayer that this vital mission of the church will become an integral part of the mission program throughout Christendom and that this essential challenge to the church will not be neglected.

Although the consumption of alcoholic beverages is decreasing somewhat, the problems of alcoholism and alcohol abuse continue unabated. An area of prime concern for the church community is the alcohol used by our young people—our next adult generation. Their first drink is being taken earlier and earlier—even as children. It is no secret that thoughtless beer consumption (the beer often being supplied by adults) by high-schoolers is widespread and the cause of many tragic automobile-accident deaths and lifelong impairments. Concomitantly, on many college and university campuses beer drinking is de rigueur and often a major contributor to problems and misdeeds (if not *crimes*) on the campus, to say nothing of low grades and incipient alcoholism.

Nevertheless, in this regard there are some bright "points of light." Preventive education is being done in many schools at all grades. College students and administrators are recognizing these problems on their campuses and are taking steps to control them. The liquor industry, feeling the heat of public opinion, is fighting back as victories are won—such as the requirement for warning labels on their products—and in the face of criticism of the flagrant advertising and sponsorship on television of sports and other events. AA and alcoholism treatment centers are seeing many younger people in their 30s, 20s and even teens coming to find sobriety—to kick their alcohol addiction and, in many cases, multi-addiction with other drugs.

Also, as interest grows in healthful living-styles, there appears to be a conscious lessening of alcohol imbibing. In recent scientific research a gene may have been found which will enable identification in advance of persons who are at risk for alcoholism, so that these persons will take no alcoholic beverages.

But there is still much to be done!

The war on illicit drugs has generated much interest, if not much success at this point, but unfortunately, this has overshadowed the much greater problem of alcohol abuse and alcoholism which in the face of some decrease in the use of illicit drugs has possibly increased. "It's only alcohol!"

The challenge to the church to do something is still very much present. The real solution remains the spiritual message which leads all to fullness of life for all who will hear and accept it.

The Apostle Paul prays for all of us:

> *that out of the treasures of his glory he may grant you strength and power through his Spirit in your inner being, that through faith, Christ may dwell in your hearts in love . . . so may you attain to the fullness of being, the fullness of God himself.*[62]

The Psalmist elucidates for those needing help:

> *Bless the Lord, my soul . . .*
> *He pardons all my guilt*
> *and heals all my suffering.*
> *He rescues me from the pit of death*
> *and surrounds me with constant love, with tender affection;*
> *He contents me with all good in the prime of life,*
> *and my youth is ever new like an eagle's.*[63]

So to all of us who care, the time is ripe to:

Hear this call—Stand up—Get moving!

[62] Ephesians 3:16, 17, 19.
[63] Psalm 103:2-5.

Appendix ❖

I. Outline for Study / Syllabus

One imperative for this text is an outline of those issues with which anyone who wants to be knowledgeable about alcohol problems and its related ministry should be familiar. Though there is an ample selection of published materials on alcoholism, there does not appear to be a concise, easy-to-use annotated syllabus. The following list includes sources where information can be found which is reliable and comprehensive. The authors noted here have a wide range of knowledge and experience which will benefit anyone ministering in this area.

It is vital to build a library of basic books and other resources to facilitate one's ministry with alcohol problems. Many of these texts are available through public libraries—either on the shelves of your local library, or available through the extensive Inter-Library System which allows local libraries to borrow widely from one another. Many universities or colleges are well-stocked in good resources on alcohol problems. Other choice sources are local affiliates of the National Council on Alcoholism, county or city alcohol programs, school programs and treatment programs—all of which may have books, videos or films which they are willing to lend.

The following syllabus is listed here by specific subjects. Included are a few questions to stimulate thinking and to help apply these issues to local situations. The first compilation is a list of the books and other publications which are basic to the subject (marked by an *) plus others that are useful and will help give you a rounded picture. Complete bibliographic information of this annotated list is included in the books listed and is also found in Appendix IV. Most of these titles are available through your local bookstore or from the publishing houses (addresses are found in Appendix IV).

Although there is some overlapping information in these titles, they each have a distinctive perspective that makes the entire list of benefit.

Basic Reading List

Alcohol and Research World, Fall 1984, Fall 1985, Fall 1987, Winter 1986-87. Quarterly published by the

National Institute on Alcohol Abuse and Alcoholism.

*Alcoholics Anonymous, "The Big Book" (Third Edition). The "bible" of AA. Must be read to understand AA.

*Stephen P. Apthorp, Alcohol and Substance Abuse. The experience and insights of an Episcopal priest.

The Bottom Line, Fall 1986, Fall 1987, Winter 1988. Excellent quarterly of up-to-date information.

*Howard J. Clinebell, Jr., Understanding and Counselling the Alcoholic (revised and enlarged, 1978). A standard text for clergy and laity.

Paul C. Conley and Andrew A. Sorensen, The Staggering Steeple. A unique history and commentary on alcohol and the church with an excellent chapter on drinking among Afro-Americans.

R. Margaret Cork, The Forgotten Children, A classic to read and weep.

John A. Ewing and Beatrice A. Rouse, eds., Drinking Alcohol in American Society—Issues and Current Research. A series of informative essays.

*Edith Lisansky Gomberg, Helene Raskin White and John A. Carpenter, eds., Alcohol, Science and Society Revisited. Excellent current essays.

Robert L. Hammond, Almost All You Ever Wanted to Know About Alcohol *but didn't know who to ask (Revised 1985). A comprehensive, readable and usable summary.

*Vernon E. Johnson, D.D., I'll Quit Tomorrow. A pioneer who popularized the intervention method for getting alcoholics into treatment.

Mark Edwards Lender, James Kirby Martin, Drinking in America. A good history which explores what is behind many of today's attitudes.

*James R. Milam and Katherine Ketcham, Under the Influence. An up-to-date "Guide to the Myths and Realities of Alcoholism."

*James E. Royce, Ph.D., Alcohol Problems and Alcoholism. An outstanding authority who teaches at Seattle University.

Marian Sandmaier, The Invisible Alcoholic. A fascinating history of alcoholism and drinking among women.

*Sixth Special Report to the U.S. Congress on Alcohol and

Health (1987), Secretary of Health and Human Services. Documentary on developments in the alcohol research and treatment fields.

*Anderson Spickard, M.D. and Barbara R. Thompson, *Dying for a Drink.* Very readable. A physician who is a Christian discusses why knowledge and training about alcoholism is necessary in medicine and the church.

*Janet Geringer Woititz, *Adult Children of Alcoholics.* One of the first and already a classic.

*Geraldine Youcha, *A Dangerous Pleasure.* A must book about women alcoholics!

As you read these basic texts there are a few points to keep in mind:

1. Try to differentiate alcohol use, alcoholism and other alcohol abuse for in much writing there is often little indication of these differences. Although information may apply to more than one of these facets, it is helpful to keep them sorted out.

2. Check the date of publication of each title because the accelerated pace of research, particularly in regard to alcoholism, often changes facts and conclusions.

3. Up to the present, most research and writing has dealt with white, male alcoholics and alcohol abusers, so special notice should be given those texts included here which deal specifically with women, youth, elderly and ethnic groups.

4. Each item here has its own bibliography which provides further resources. One's study will be enhanced by the addition of current magazine and journal articles found on these lists.

5. A dictionary and an encyclopedia is an asset to any library compilation to help define technical terms.

6. A notebook, organized in a convenient manner, is another tool to help keep valuable material accumulated in an accessible manner.

7. This Syllabus lists enough material to make anyone knowledgeable and able to proceed intelligently with

alcohol abuse programs, but it should be noted that certificated courses are offered at many colleges and universities which facilitate anyone to work professionally in the field.

Alcohol, Including Beverage Alcohol

In defining this substance "alcohol" with which we are concerned, we need first to realize that we find it as an important ingredient in many everyday items. To understand why it reacts with the human system as it does, we must have some basic knowledge of its chemistry. The one type of alcohol with which we are especially concerned is *beverage alcohol*—an ingredient used by the human species from the beginning of our history. Much new knowledge and even some surprises are to be found in the following.

Alcohol	*Suggested Reading*
What it is and its uses.	*World Book* or other encyclopedia.

Question: In what forms other than beverages have you used alcohol recently? Is there a future for "gasohol"?

Beverage Alcohol	*Suggested Reading*
What it is: • Chemical make-up • How it is made • Types • Congeners • Percent of alcohol in each type • What is meant by "proof"	*World Book* or other encyclopedia. James E. Royce, *Alcohol Problems and Alcoholism*, Ch. 4. James R. Milam and Katherine Ketcham, *Under the Influence,* Ch. 2.

Question: Go into a store where alcoholic beverages are sold and read a number of labels to find out what the contents of the bottles or cans are and what their alcohol content is. What more information should be supplied to the consumer?

History of Use of Beverage Alcohol	Suggested Reading
• General	Royce, Ch. 3. John A. Ewing and Beatrice A. Rouse, *Drinking Alcohol in American Society*, Chs. 1-2.
• By women	This book, Ch. 5a. Marian Sandmaier, *The Invisible Alcoholic*, Ch. 2.
• In America — General — Role of the church	Ewing & Rouse, Ch. 3 Paul C. Conley and Andrew A. Sorensen, *The Staggering Steeple.* Edith Lisansky Gomberg, Helene Raskin White and John A. Carpenter, *Alcohol, Science and Society Revisited,* pp. 355-361.
— By Afro-Americans	Conley and Sorensen, Ch. 5.
— By Native Americans	Gomberg, et al, Ch. 5 Mark Edwards Lender & James Kirby Martin, *Drinking in America,* pp. 21-26, 49-50.Mark Edwards Lender & James Kirby Martin, *Drinking in America,* pp. 21-26, 49-50.

Questions: In your experience, how have women who are drunk been perceived as compared to men who are drunk? Does the above-listed reading alter your feelings about the liquor situation among Afro-Americans and Native Americans?

Cultural Attitudes and Practices re Beverage Alcohol:	Suggested Reading
• In general in America	Gomberg, et al, Ch. 6 Ewing & Rouse, Ch. 9.
• In the churches	Gomberg, et al, pp. 361-4.
• Among multiple U.S. cultures	Gomberg, et al, pp. 66ff.
• Among Native Americans	Gomberg, et al, Ch. 5.
• Among Afro-Americans, Hispanics, Asians	Gomberg, et al, Ch. 20.
• Among minorities in general	*Alcohol, Health and Research World,* Winter 1986-87.
• Related to women	Stephen P. Apthorp, *Alcohol and Substance Abuse,* Ch. 5. Geraldine Youcha, *A Dangerous Pleasure,* Ch. 2.
• Related to elderly	Apthorp, Ch. 5.
• Related to youth	Ewing & Rouse, Chs. 10 & 11.
• In cultures elsewhere	Gomberg, et al, Ch. 4. Royce, pp. 35-38.

Question: What is the attitude toward drinking in your own cultural heritage?

Effect of Alcohol on Drinkers:	Suggested Reading
• Initial effect—depressant or stimulant? • How the body takes care of alcohol — blood alcohol level (BAL) or blood alcohol concentration (BAC) — metabolism, effect on body's organs — fetal alcohol syndrome • How it affects behavior • Potentiation or synergism	Royce, Ch. 4. Milam, Chs. 2-7. Youcha, Ch. 3. Spickard and Thompson, *Dying For a Drink,* Ch. 5 Gomberg, et al, Ch. 2. (quite technical) Royce, Ch. 5. Gomberg, et al, Ch. 3. Royce, pp. 75-76.

Questions: Have you known of someone who has suffered direct, injurious effects from alcohol ingestion? What is the BAL or BAC which your state considers intoxication, therefore making it illegal to drive?

Consumption of Beverage Alcohol:	Suggested Reading
• Patterns of drinking in the U.S. — amounts, trends	*The Bottom Line,* Fall 1987.

• Problems resulting — societal impact, e.g. youth, elderly, deaths, crime, poly-drug use	*The Bottom Line,* Fall 1986, Fall 1987. *Alcohol World,* Spring 1984 *Sixth Special Report to the U.S. Congress,* Ch. 1. Royce, pp. 75-76. Youcha, pp. 130-131.
— financial cost	*The Bottom Line,* Fall 1987.
— impact of advertising	Ibid.

Question: With the consumption of alcoholic beverages going down at present, how is the need for ministry in regard to alcohol problem affected?

A compelling quote:

How does it hurt you? According to the Drug Enforcement Administration, $400 of the price of your next new car goes to alcohol and other drug abuse: production mistakes, down-time and employee assistance programs related to alcohol and other drug problems. Similarly, the abuse of alcohol and other drugs adds $11.7 billion to our health insurance and $4 billion to workmen's compensation insurance, according to a 1986 study by the Comprehensive Care Corporation of Irvine, CA, commissioned by the CARE Institute.[64]

Question: Battles are being fought over advertising. Is the ban on advertising alcohol in the media infringing on the right to free speech?

Additional reading: Michael Jacobson, et al, *The Booze Mer-*

---

[64] Tineke B. Haase, ed., "From the Editor's Desk," *Prevention Pipeline* (Washington, DC, May/June, 1988) p. 1.

chants: The Inebriating of America.

Role of Government	Suggested Reading
• History, laws and taxation • Policy development & NIAAA	Royce, Ch. 20. Ewing and Rouse, Chs. 14, 18. Gomberg, et al, Ch. 23.

Question: Since alcohol use is legal, should the use of "hard drugs" also be allowed?

Alcoholism

Alcoholism is one of the most intriguing and at the same time one of the most tragic conditions afflicting humanity. Almost universally condemned, it is more misunderstood than understood; feared, yet courted with nonchalance. There is no recovery, but daily vigilance—one-day-at-a-time, in the company of others who are like-affected—gives joy in living and renewed productivity.

Fortunately, today we are living in a time when empirical insight has led to much positive interest and serious research to find answers to the why? what? how? and what now? of alcoholism.

Alcoholism	Suggested Reading
What is it? Compose a definition of your own.	Royce, Ch. 1. Milam, pp. 168-171) Gomberg, et al, Ch. 7. (Quite technical)

Question: How valid is the saying: "Alcoholism is something you have, drinking is something you do"?

Alcoholism As a Disease	*Suggested Reading*
• History	Ewing & Rouse, Ch. 3.
	Youcha, Ch. 5.
• Pros and cons	Royce, Ch. 10.
• Is it a sin?	Apthorp, Ch. 4.
	Spickard, pp. 40-41.
• Relation to "respon-	Milam, pp. 173- 174.
sible drinking"	This book, Ch. 7.

Question: Should churches try to regulate the drinking habits of their parishioners?

The *causes of alcoholism* are still a matter of much research. They are dealt with extensively in many of the works cited. Of special note are those by Royce, Spickard, Milam, Youcha, Clinebell and Apthorp. (Look in their indices for relevant material.) Beyond the mere complexity of alcoholism, note the enabling causality factors involving socio-cultural, psychological and physical issues as well as the spiritual questions related to alcoholism. An additional source is the pioneer researcher Donald Goodwin's, *Is Alcoholism Hereditary?*

Again, when looking at the typical *characteristics of alcoholism* (as differentiated from the *causes*) one must look beyond the obvious symptoms to those complex physical, behavioral, mental, emotional and social patterns which although having some commonality are manifested differently in each person.

Characteristics of Alcoholism	*Suggested Reading*
• Intoxication—taken for granted, but not always obvious	Royce, pp. 16-17.
	Milam, Chs. 4-7.
• In the early, middle and late stages	Royce, Ch. 6.

	Vernon Johnson, D.D., *I'll Quit Tomorrow*, Chs. 1-4. Spickard, Ch. 6. Ewing and Rouse, Ch. 4.
• Denial	Apthorp, pp. 69-70. Spickard, Chs. 7-8.
• Alcohol as the solution	Clinebell, p. 69.
• Cross-addiction	Royce, pp. 75-76 Milam, Ch. 10.
• Spiritual decline	Royce, Ch. 18. Spickard, p. 43. Johnson, Chs. 1-4; Clinebell, Ch. 6.
• In special groups — women — youth — ethnic groups — homosexuals — military — professions — skid row — elderly	Royce, Ch. 7. Gomberg, et al, Chs. 19-20 Milam, pp. 39-41. Sandmaier, Chs. 4-10. Youcha, pp. 107-108.

Question: One of the most unfortunate aspects of alcoholism is the ignorance of families, friends and employers about the disease. What behaviors might be a tip-off that a drinking problem is alcoholism?

The *scope of alcoholism* is hard to ascertain. Consistent statistics on alcoholism are, by the nature of the disease, difficult to find because the exact number of alcoholics in the population cannot be determined when so many victims do not admit to it. Beyond this, there is widespread mis-reporting of alcoholism when it is involved in other medical problems and deaths. The following figures thus represent current findings, but it must be stated there is a need for much more research and refinement. The enormity of the problem—first in morbidity (troublesomeness)—in our society is agreed to by all sources.

In the United States it is variously considered to be the third or fourth highest cause of death. Joseph Califano, former Secretary of Health, Education and Welfare, states that it is involved in five of the ten leading causes of untimely death, e.g., cancer, accidents, cirrhosis of the liver, suicide and homicide.[65]

Statistics on Alcoholism	Suggested Reading
• In the U.S. — estimated numbers of alcoholics — number seeking treatment — hospital population — women • Human cost to society, family, women and children — adult children — fetal alcohol syndrome • Financial costs	Royce, Ch. 2. *Bottom Line,* Fall 1987, p. 26. *Bottom Line,* Winter 1988, p. 29. *Alcohol World,* Fall 1987, p. 10—insert. Youcha, pp. 170-171. Gomberg, et al, pp. 143-147. Royce, Ch. 8. Youcha, Ch. 8. Margaret Cork, *The Forgotten Children* Janet Geringer Woititz, *Adult Children of Alcoholics* Youcha, Ch. 9. Royce, pp. 65-66. Milam, pp. 38-39. *Alcohol World,* Fall 1985 Ibid., Fall 1987, pp. 10-15

Questions: What sort of statistics do your local authorities keep in regard to alcohol-involved problems in your

---

[65] Joseph Califano, *America's Health Care Revolution* (New York, Random House, 1986) pp. 71, 188,

area and the cost to the taxpayers of such problems? Have you known any children who exhibit behavior that may indicate they come from an alcoholic home?

Dangers of Alcoholism	Suggested Reading
• To alcoholics — Physical, behavioral, economic and spiritual problems • accidents	Milam, Chs. 4-6. Spickard, Ch. 6. Johnson, Chs. 1-4.

Additional reading: Emanuel Peluso and Lucy Silvay Peluso, *Women and Drugs*

Treatment	Suggested Reading

• Background
 	
• Goals
• Elements in treatment
  — holistic
  — detoxification
  — tranquilizers
  — antabuse
  — special needs
  — cross-addictions
  — family involvement
  — co-dependency
  — Al-Anon and Alateen
  — adult children
	Spickard, Ch. 17.
	Apthorp, pp. 147-149.
	Milam, pp. 124-134.
	Royce, Ch. 14.
	Spickard, Chs. 17-18.
	Johnson, Chs. 7-10.
	Milam, pp. 134-151.
	Gomberg, et al, Ch. 15.
	Alcohol World, Fall 1986.
	Youcha, Ch. 10.
	Milam, Ch. 10
	Spickard, Ch. 21,
	Clinebell, Ch. 11.
	Apthorp, pp. 115-118.
	Royce, Ch. 16.
	
	Apthorp, pp. 138-142.

• New life building – commitment – AA participation – spiritual – physical – everyday living skills • relapse	Royce, Chs. 15 & 17. Spickard, Ch. 19-20. Milam, pp. 136-152. Johnson, Ch. 12. *Big-Book,* pp. 47ff. Royce, pp. 277-278. Spickard, Ch. 22.

The terms "recovery," "recovering," "arrested" and "remission" are frequently used interchangeably. Since there is no actual recovery from alcoholism at the present time, that term is in error. The others are permissible with "recovering" used by AA members as a rule.

Treatment Programs	*Suggested Reading*
• Alcoholics Anonymous • Inpatient – medical model – social model • Outpatient • Costs	Royce, Ch. 15. Apthorp, pp. 130-136. Gomberg, et al, Ch. 17. *Big Book* Spickard, pp. 136-139. Royce, p. 229. Milam, pp. 134-152. Clinebell, chaps. 8-10. *Alcohol World,* Fall 1987, pp. 10-11. Gomberg, et al, Ch. 23.

For a realistic assessment of current costs, inquire at local or nearby treatment centers in your area.

Question: Since many who need treatment do not have health insurance and do not qualify for government funds that would pay even a modest amount for treatment, what suggestions can be given the alcoholic person who needs professional help?

Choosing a treatment program	Suggested Reading
• Factors to consider: — treatment needed — facilities available — ownership, administration — quality of program — cost	Royce, pp. 213-215. Milam, pp. 110-111. Apthorp, pp. 150-151. Youcha, pp. 190ff.

Not many treatment services are run directly by churches or other religious organizations; however, a large number of people operating such facilities are Christian and have church affiliation. Although the religious aspect is important, by far the overriding factor is whether those operating the facility understand alcoholics and work genuinely for their recovery. If this is the case, there is a viable chance that the recovering alcoholic's spiritual recovery will begin and develop well.

How to accomplish getting the alcoholic into treatment is always an anguished question, yet this, in fact, is the key problem the family, friends or employer must face.

Getting the Alcoholic into Treatment.	Suggested Reading
• Preparation — roles of family, employer, friends, school, church — identifying available services • The intervention process	Royce, Ch. 13. Spickard, Chs. 13 & 14. Milam, Ch. 8. Clinebell, pp. 196-211. Apthorp, pp. 143-152 AA literature Spickard, Chs. 15 & 16. Johnson, Ch. 5 & 6.

• The intervention process • Myths about treatment • Government involvement	Royce, pp. 215-217. Youcha, pp. 170-177. Apthorp, pp. 103-126. Spickard, Ch. 13. Milam, pp. 12-15. Ewing & Rouse, Ch. 17. Gomberg, et al, Ch. 23.

Question: Who in your community can give expert help in setting up an intervention or help care for a family while the alcoholic member—father or mother—is away in treatment?

Additional readings: Harold E. Hughes, *The Man From Ida Grove* and Carolyn L. Weiner, *Politics of Alcohol.*

Alcohol Abuse

In addition to alcoholism, the other significant area of alcohol problems is well called *alcohol abuse.* This aspect of alcohol use is the cause, or a contributing cause, of much distress, yet it is virtually neglected as a specific area of concern.

Read Chapter 7 again, then:

1. List examples of alcohol abuse which you have observed or learned about.
2. Decide which crimes listed in Table 10 (p. 13) of the *6th Special Report to Congress* might have been committed by alcoholics or by moderate to heavy drinkers.

Question: How do you rate the success of the current emphasis on avoiding driving after drinking? How could excessive drinking be controlled on pleasure boats or private aircraft?

Prevention

Prevention is an important area of concern. From our earliest days we are trained by our parents, teachers and others in a thousand ways to prevent injuries to ourselves and others. Our lives are circumscribed by society's laws and regulations which are designed to prevent catastrophe.

Yet often effective prevention is elusive in the use of alcoholic beverages. Even when it might be within legal limits, there is still much misuse of alcohol which results in serious societal problems. For these reasons, prevention of alcohol abuse must be seriously considered and diligently pursued if we are going to make headway in the current "war on drugs".

Fortunately the church is uniquely positioned to do effective prevention:

- It has the spiritual message which equips one to resist abusing alcohol and also enables successful sobriety.
- It can call individuals, communities or the nation to examine the impact of the use of alcohol and it can influence action in its regard.
- It has a ready-made network of able leaders (including clergy) and an educational system which reaches into every city, town and rural hamlet.
- The clergy and other leaders are able to reach out without intimidation to all ages both within and outside their local congregations offering assistance and healing.
- It has access to other helping services and professional people.

Questions: In what ways do you see your local congregation being positioned to do prevention? Allen Luks in his book, *Will America Sober Up?*[66] says that in the 1980s the nation realized alcohol was by far its greatest drug problem. Is this statement still valid?

---

[66] Boston: Beacon Press, 1983, p. 3.

After many years of being virtually ignored, prevention has recently become a serious issue both in relation to the use of alcohol and of other drugs. Amazingly, in 1986 alcohol and other drug abuse cost $850 per capita in the United States, while only 77¢ per person was spent on the prevention of such abuse![67] An increasing number of articles and books are now surfacing on prevention, and numerous training courses and workshops are being offered throughout the nation. The variety of passages cited below reflect the newness of the movement.

Prevention	Suggested Reading

• History
  — prohibition
  — temperance movement
  — new temperance movement
• Goals
  — include *alcohol abuse*
  — integrated
• Primary prevention
  — spiritual and holistic
  — public health model
  — education
  — advertising laws and regulations
	Gomberg, et al, Ch. 24.
	
	Conley and Sorensen, Ch. 3-5.
	Lender and Martin, Ch.4.
	
	Royce, pp. 180-181.
	6th Report to Congress, p. 97.
	
	Royce, p. 181.
	
	6th Report to Congress, pp. 102-109.

Primary prevention—which includes whatever factors may help keep a person from becoming harmfully involved with alcohol or other drugs—is, indeed, the bastion of the church. It is here that a spiritual and holistic approach to prevention will

---

[67] Haase, loc. cit.

help determine whether or not one gets into trouble with mood-altering substances.

The community must also take an active role in the primary prevention process, for the community as a whole suffers when alcohol is abused by members of the society. A world expert on prevention, Dr. Ernest Noble, has said,

> Of all prevention measures, regulating the supply of alcoholic beverages is the most direct and effective means of dealing with alcohol consumption and its associated harms. . . . The primary underlying basis for state alcohol control codes is the prevention of alcohol abuse and the promotion of temperance.[68]

Additional readings: Allen Luks, *Will America Sober Up?* Ch. 1; and Michael Jacobson, et al, *The Booze Merchants.*

• Secondary prevention	
— interrupt and reverse course of problem drinking	6th Report to Congress, p. 109
	Clinebell, pp. 306-309
— training in recognition of problems	
— key role of denial	Apthorp, pp. 69-70
• Children of alcoholics (28 million)	Spickard, Chs. 7-8.
	6th Report to Congress, pp. 111-112.
— highest risk group to develop alcoholism	Milam, pp. 36-39
	Woititz, p. 103
— dysfunctional lives of adult children	Apthorp, pp. 139-143.
• Costs	
	Gomberg, et al, Ch. 23.

[68] In an address given to the 6th World Prevention Conference, 1986, Nice, France, (reported in *Bottom Line,* Fall, 1986, pp. 8-10).

It is important that a focused educational campaign be implemented to make it possible for the average person to recognize drinking problems when they are encountered, be able to respond intelligently to such predicaments and know how and where to refer people for treatment.

This is doubly necessary for groups such as health care providers, educators, counsellors, truant officers, administrators, student leaders, management personnel, clergy, church lay-leaders, social workers, legal system personnel including lawyers, judges, law officers and parole officers. It makes common sense that all such receive training as a matter of course in their professional or specialized education. Community workshops, sponsored by civic agencies, clinics, hospitals *and churches* can explain prevention and treatment programs to a wide array of the populace. Here discussions of abstinence, life-restructuring and recovery programs could invite serious participation from those needing such help, plus provide family members necessary support groups.

A word about *denial,* the maddening, common denominator permeating all types of alcohol problems. "Nobody here has a drinking problem!" is the cry. Frequently such denial is recognized in hindsight, but it tends to be a very strong element in the early stages of alcoholism and other alcohol abuse situations—both by the alcoholic / abuser and by those around them. To intervene effectively and prevent further deterioration, such denial must be dashed.

Questions: What types of support groups for children and for adult children of alcoholics are available in your community? What are the churches in your community doing to participate in local prevention measures?

Additional reading: Robert L. DuPont, Jr., *Getting Tough on Gateway Drugs.*

II. List of Contributors of Ideas for Ministry
(Indicated by § in text)

These are the names of the persons who sent ideas for alcohol ministry in reply to my informal survey as I began this book. Also included are the names of several others who communicated to me their concern about this ministry and in many cases told of their own efforts to meet the need where they were. Many of the latter appeared in the *Alcohol Network News,* the newsletter of the Presbyterian Network on Alcohol and Other Drug Abuse (PNAODA) while I was editor.

I thank all of these persons whose names appear for their inspiration and many more whom I cannot name. My prayers for each of your ministries, that they may continue and prosper as lives are changed.

§1. *Rev. Bob Adams*
§2. *John Arnold*
§3. *Rev. Florence Beaujon*
§4. *Rev. Don Bell*
§5. *"Ben"*
§6. *Ila K. Bench*
§7. *Rev. Edwin D. Bernard*
§8. *Rev. Steven Boots*
§9. *Gary Borgeson and Carol Hacker*
§10. *Loel Millar Buckley*
§11. *Rev. Carnegie S. Calian*
§12. *Jane Campbell*
§13. *Rev. Vern R. Campbell*
§14. *James H. Clipson, Jr.*
§15. *Linda Clough*
§16. *Hester M. Cochran*
§17. *Jennifer Cochran (pen name)*
§18. *Frederick B. Cooley*
§19. *Dan F. Coughlin*
§20. *Ted Cowan*

§21. *Rev. W. T. Cunningham*
§22. *Rev. John H. Davis*
§23. *Rev. George DeHority, Jr.*
§24. *Rev. David Dilworth*
§25. *Ovida Dorr*
§26. *Betty Null Eskridge*
§27. *Rev. Kenneth Fells*
§28. *Rev. Bob Field*
§29. *Lois O. Flanigan*
§30. *Rev. Clark Fobes*
§31. *Rev. Mike Gibson*
§32. *Rev. Richard W. Gillespie*
§33. *Jonathan E. Gradess*
§34. *Rev. Dennis J. Haines*
§35. *Marianne Hall*
§36. *Veronica Hall*
§37. *Rev. David C. Hancock*
§38. *Rev. William B. Harnish*
§39. *Dave Heil*
§40. *Lois Bond Johnson*

§41. Trent Jones
§42. Estele Keating
§43. Rev. Rollin D. Kirk
§44. Roger C. Kissel
§45. Mrs. Frank H. Layne
§46. Mona Logan
§47. Rev. Tanta Luck-
hardt-Davis
§48. Rev. Don Maddox
§49. Rev. Barry McCabe
§50. Ruth McCullough
§51. Rev. Frank McDowell
§52. Rev. David McGown
§53. Sharon McLeod
§54. Rev. Robert C. McNeil
§55. Rev. David McShane
§56. Rev. George L. Miller
§57. Betty M. Minemeir
§58. Suzanne Morse
§59. Rev. James Nelson
§60. Rev. John (Jack)
Newell
§61. David Olson
§62. Bob Osborne
§63. Rev. Jay Paris
§64. Joe Partansky
§65. Katherine Pearson
§66. Donna L. Porter
§67. Rev. Jeffrey Earl
Porter
§68. Lois Potter
§69. Ken and Evelyn R.
Potts
§70. Rev. Dick Prosser
§71. Rev. Ransom Rice
§72. Robert E. Romanelli
§73. Rev. Stephen Sapp
§74. Rev. William W.
Satterwhite

§75. Eleanore Schafer
§76. Pat Schlichting
§77. Rev. John D. Sharick
§78. Rev. L. Shaw
§79. Joan Shellene
§80. Rev. Doyle Shields
§81. Rev. John Sinclair
§82. David R. Smith
§83. Jacqueline McCalla
Smith
§84. Rev. Roger Smith
§85. Rev. John Spahr
§86. Rev. Elwood E.
Spence
§87. Rev. Lowell H.
Spencer
§88. Anderson Spickard,
M.D.
§89. Rev. Charles Stewart
§90. Dona Marie Swain
§91. Rev. William J.
Tammen
§92. Barbara Z. Tilton
§93. Sarah Todd
§94. Rev. Ernest Tune
§95. Rev. Raymond L.
White
§96. Rev. William B. White
§97. Rev. Tom Wilbanks
§98. Rev. William Wilcox
§99. Rev. Hannibal A. Williams
§100. Nora M. Wilson
§101. Rev. Diana Vezmar-
Bailey
§102. Rev. David Works
§103. Rev. Warren Zeh
§104. Anonymous
§105. Anonymous

III. The Twelve Steps of Alcoholics Anonymous

1. We admitted we were powerless over alcohol—that our lives had become unmanageable.
2. Came to believe that a Power greater than ourselves could restore us to sanity.
3. Made a decision to turn our will and our lives over to the care of God *as we understood Him.*
4. Made a searching and fearless moral inventory of ourselves.
5. Admitted to God, to ourselves and to another human being the exact nature of our wrongs.
6. Were entirely ready to have God remove all these defects of character.
7. Humbly asked Him to remove our shortcomings.
8. Made a list of all persons we had harmed and became willing to make amends to them all.
9. Made direct amends to such people wherever possible, except when to do so would injure them or others.
10. Continued to take personal inventory and when we were wrong promptly admitted it.
11. Sought through prayer and meditation to improve our conscious contact with God *as we understood Him,* praying only for knowledge of God's will for us and the power to carry that out.
12. Having had a spiritual awakening as the result of these steps, we tried to carry this message to alcoholics and to practice these principles in all our affairs.

(The Twelve Steps are reprinted with permission of Alcoholics Anonymous World Services, Inc. Permission to reprint this material does not mean that AA has reviewed or approved the contents of this publication nor that AA agrees with views expressed herein. AA is a program of recovery from alcoholism—use of the Twelve Steps in connection with programs and activities patterned after AA, but which address other problems, does not imply otherwise.)

IV. Resources

1. Books

Alcohol and Alcoholism

Bell, Peter. *Chemical Dependency and the African-American.* Center City, MN: Hazelden.

Bissell, Le Clair and Paul Haberman. *Alcoholism in the Professions.* New York: Oxford University Press, 1984. (Includes a rare report of alcoholism among the clergy [pp. 158-162].)

Ewing, John A. and Beatrice Rouse, (eds.). *Drinking, Alcohol in American Society—Issues and Current Research.* Chicago: Nelson-Hall, 1978.

Fitzgerald, Kathleen Whalen. *Alcoholism, the Genetic Inheritance.* New York: Doubleday, 1988.

Fort, Joel. *Our Biggest Drug Problem.* New York: McGraw-Hill, 1973.

Gilmore, Thomas B. *Equivocal Spirits—Alcoholism and Drinking in Twentieth Century Literature.* Chapel Hill, NC: University of North Carolina Press, 1987.

Gomberg, Edith Lisansky, Helene Raskin White and John A. Carpenter, (eds.). *Alcohol, Science and Society Revisited.* Ann Arbor, MI: University of Michigan Press, 1982.

Goodwin, Donald W. *Alcoholism: The Facts.* New York: Oxford University Press, 1981.

Goodwin, Donald W. *Is Alcoholism Hereditary?* New York: Oxford University Press, 1976.

Jellinek, E. M. *The Disease Concept of Alcoholism.* New Haven, CT: College and University Press, 1960.

Johnson, Vernon. *Everything You Need To Know About Chemical Dependence.* Minneapolis: Johnson Institute, 1990.

Kane, Geoffrey P. *Inner-City Alcoholism.* New York: Human Services Press, 1981. (Drawn from case work in the Bronx. Unusual chapter on "Culture and Alcoholism: Blacks and Hispanics".)

Keller, Mark. *A Historical Overview of Alcohol and Alco-*

holism. Reprint from Cancer Research, Vol. 39, July 1979. Piscataway, NJ: Rutgers Center of Alcohol Studies.

Keller, Mark, Mairi McCormick and Vera Efron. *Dictionary of Words About Alcohol, 2nd Ed.* Piscataway, NJ: Rutgers Center of Alcohol Studies, 1982.

Lender, Mark Edward and James Kirby Martin. *Drinking in America.* New York: The Free Press/Macmillan, 1982.

McCarthy, Raymond Gerald, (ed.). *Drinking and Intoxication.* Glencoe, IL: Free Press, 1959.

Milam, James R. and Katherine Ketcham. *Under the Influence.* Seattle: Madrona Publishers, Inc., 1981 (also in Bantam Books).

Nellis, Muriel. *The Female Fix.* Boston: Houghton-Mifflin, 1980.

Peluso, Emanuel and Lucy Silvay Peluso. *Women and Drugs.* Minneapolis: CompCare Publishers, 1988.

Pittman, D. J. and E. P. Snyder (eds.). *Society, Culture and Drinking Patterns.* New York: John Wiley & Sons, 1962. (Excellent background chapter by Selden Bacon entitled: "Alcohol and Complex Society".)

Royce, James E. *Alcohol Problems and Alcoholism, A Comprehensive Survey.* New York: The Free Press/ Macmillan, 1981.

Rohrbaugh, W. J. *The Alcoholic Republic.* New York: Oxford Press, 1979.

Rudy, D.R. *Becoming Alcoholic: Alcoholics Anonymous and the Reality of Alcoholism.* Edwardsville, IL: Southern Illinois University Press, 1986.

Sandmaier, Marian. *The Invisible Alcoholics.* New York: McGraw-Hill, 1980.

Smithers Foundation. *Understanding Alcoholism.* New York: Charles Scribner and Sons, 1968.

Spradley, James P. *You Owe Yourself a Drunk.* Boston: Little, Brown & Co., 1970. (An ethnograph of urban nomads.)

Trice, Harrison H. and Paul M. Roman. *Spirits and Demons at Work: Alcohol and Other Drugs on the Job.* Ithaca, NY: New York State School of Industrial and Labor Relations, 1979.

Twerski, Abraham J. *It Happens to Doctors, Too.* Center

City, MN: Hazelden, 1982.

U.S. Department of Health and Human Services. *6th Special Report to the U.S. Congress on Alcohol and Health, 1987.* (Available from National Clearinghouse for Alcohol and Drug Information, P.O. Box 2345, Rockville, MD, 20852.)

U.S. Department of Health and Human Services. *7th Special Report to the U.S. Congress on Alcohol and Health, 1990.* (Available same as above.)

Vaillant, George E. *The Natural History of Alcoholism.* Cambridge MA: Harvard University Press, 1983.

Wiseman, Jacqueline P. *Stations of the Lost, The Treatment of Skid Row Alcoholics.* Englewood Cliffs, NJ: Prentice-Hall, 1970.

Youcha, Geraldine. *A Dangerous Pleasure: Alcohol From the Woman's Perspective.* New York: Hawthorn Books, 1978.

Ziebold, Thomas O. and John Mongeon (eds.). *Alcoholism and Homosexuality.* New York: Haworth Press, 1982.

Treatment and Recovery

Alcoholics Anonymous. *Alcoholics Anonymous: "The Big Book"* (Third Edition). New York: Alcoholics Anonymous World Services, Inc., 1976; 10th printing, 1981.

Alcoholics Anonymous. *Living Sober.* New York: Alcoholics Anonymous World Services, Inc., 1975.

Alcoholics Anonymous. *Twelve Steps and Twelve Traditions, Bill W.'s 24 Essays on Recovery.* New York: Alcoholics Anonymous World Services, Inc. nd.

Anderson, Daniel J. *Perspectives on Treatment: The Minnesota Experience.* Center City, MN: Hazelden, 1981.

Brisbane, Frances Larry and Maxine Womble (eds.). *Treatment of Black Alcoholics.* New York: Haworth Press, 1985. (Excellent on spirituality.)

De Jong, Alexander C. *Help and Hope for the Alcoholic.* Wheaton, IL: Tyndale House 1982.

Finnegan, Dana and Emily McNally. *Counselling Chemically Dependent Gay Men and Lesbians.* Center City, MN: Hazelden.

Fishel, Ruth. *The Journey Within.* Pompano Beach, FL:

Health Communications, 1987.

Greenwood, Morgan, et al (ed.). *Social Model Recovery: An Alternative to Traditional Clinical Treatment.* Burbank, CA: Bridge Focus, Inc., 1990.

Hansen, Philip L. *The Afflicted and the Affected.* Minneapolis: Park Printing, 1974.

———, *Sick and Tired of Being Sick and Tired.* Minneapolis: Park Printing, 1980.

Johnson, Vernon E. *I'll Quit Tomorrow.* New York: Harper and Row, 1973. (A classic on progression of alcoholism and intervention.)

Johnson, Vernon E. *Intervention: How To Help Someone Who Doesn't Want Help.* Minneapolis: Johnson Institute, 1986.

Kurtz, Ernest. *Not God: A History of Alcoholics Anonymous.* Center City, MN: Hazelden, 1979.

Mann, Marty. *Marty Mann's New Primer on Alcoholism.* New York: Holt, Rinehart and Winston, 1981.

Nale, Sharon, edited by Barbara Kortrey. *A Cry For Help.* Philadelphia: Fortress Press, 1982.

Shields, Des and Ann Shields. *How to Love Yourself and Everybody Else.* Ventura, CA: Agape Center (7322 Ralston St., 93003)

Twerski, Abraham J. *Addictive Thinking.* Center City, MN: Hazelden, 1990.

U.S. Department of Health and Human Services, National Institute of Alcoholism and Alcohol Abuse. *A Guide to Planning Alcohol-Treatment Programs.* (No. 017-024-01277-7) Washington, DC, Superintendent of Documents.

Treatment Directories

National Women's Directory. 1988. Human Services Institute, 512 - 33 St. Ct. West, Bradenton, Fl 34202.

Moore, Jean (ed.). *Roads to Recovery: A National Directory.* New York: Collier Books/Macmillan, 1985.

Children and Family

Ackerman, Robert J. *Children of Alcoholics,* 2nd Edition.

Holmes Beach, FL: Learning Publications, 1978.

Ackerman, Robert J. *Perfect Daughters.* Deerfield Beach, FL: Health Communication, 1989.

Al-Anon. *The Dilemma of the Alcoholic Marriage.* New York: Al-Anon Family Groups, 1984.

Al-Anon. *Living with an Alcoholic.* New York: Al-Anon Family Groups, 1985. (History and purpose of Al-Anon.)

Beatie, Melody. *Co-Dependent No More.* Center City, MN: Hazelden, 1987.

Black, Claudia. *It Will Never Happen to Me.* Denver, CO: M.A.C. Printing and Publications Division, 1982.

Bowden, Julie and Herbert Gravitz. *Genesis. Spirituality in Recovery from Childhood Traumas.* Deerfield Beach, FL: Health Communications, 1988.

Bratton, Mary. *A Guide to Family Intervention.* Deerfield Beach, FL: Health Communications, 1987.

Brooks, Cathleen. *The Secret Everyone Knows.* Center City, MN: Hazelden/Cork 1981.

Carl, Cecil E., *Letters to Elderly Alcoholics.* Center City, MN: Hazelden, 1980.

Cork, Margaret. *The Forgotten Children.* Toronto: Alcohol and Drug Addiction Research Foundation, 1980.

Dalmetsch, Paul and Gail Mauricette, (eds.). *Teens Talk About Alcohol and Alcoholism.* Garden City, NY: Doubleday & Co., 1987. (A compilation of essays written by students of Mt. Anthony Union Junior High School, Bennington, VT.)

Deutsch, Charles. *Broken Bottles, Broken Dreams: Understanding and Helping the Children of Alcoholics.* New York: Teachers College Press, 1982.

Drews, Toby Rice. *Getting Them Sober, Vols. I, II, & III.* Plainfield. NJ: Hover Books, 1980. (Recommended by "Dear Abby".)

DuPont, Jr., Robert L. *Getting Tough on Gateway Drugs, A Guide for the Family.* Washington, DC: American Psychiatric Press, 1985.

Hacker, Michael. *Winthrop and Munchie Talk About Alcohol.* Center City, MN: Hazelden/Cork, 1983. (A children's coloring book.)

Hornick, Edith Lynn. *Teenagers Guide to Living With An*

Alcoholic Parent. Center City, MN: Hazelden, 1984.

Joachim, Kitty. *Spirituality and Chemical Dependency: Guidelines for Treatment.* New York: Oxford University Press, 1988.

Krupski, Ann Marie. *Inside the Adolescent Alcoholic.* Center City, MN: Hazelden, 1982.

Lagone, John. *Bombed, Buzzed, Smashed or Sober.* Boston: Little, Brown, 1976 (also in Avon Paperbacks).

Martin, Sara Hines. *Healing For Adult Children of Alcoholics.* Nashville, TN: Broadman Press, 1988.

Maxwell, Ruth. *The Booze Battle,* New York: Ballantine Paperbacks, 1986.

McCabe, Thomas R. *Victims No More.* Center City, MN: Hazelden, 1978.

Robe, Lucy Barry. *Just So It's Healthy.* Minneapolis: CompCare Publishers, 1982. (Excellent bibliography.)

Robinson, Bryan E. *Work Addiction—Hidden Legacies of Adult Children.* Deerfield Beach, FL: Health Communications, 1989.

Schaef, Anne Wilson. *Co-Dependence, Misunderstood-Mistreated.* San Francisco: Harper and Row, 1983.

Seixas, Judith S. and Geraldine Youcha. *Children of Alcoholism, A Survivors Manual.* New York: Harper and Row, 1985.

Smith, Ann W. *Grandchildren of Alcoholics.* Deerfield Beach, FL: Health Communications, 1988.

U.S. Department of Health and Human Services. *A Growing Concern—How to Provide Services for Children from Alcoholic Families.* (DHHS Pub. No. [ADM]83-1257) Washington, DC: Superintendent of Documents, 1983.

Wegscheider, Sharon. *Another Chance, Hope and Health for the Alcoholic Family.* Palo Alto, CA: Science and Behavior Books, 1981.

Wegscheider-Cruse, Sharon. *Choicemaking, for Co-dependents, Adult Children and Spirituality Seekers.* Deerfield Beach, FL: Health Communications, 1985.

Wegscheider, Don. *If Only My Family Understood Me.* Minneapolis: CompCare Publishers, 1979.

Woititz, Janet Geringer. *Adult Children of Alcoholics.* Deerfield Beach, FL: Health Communications, 1983.

Woititz, Janet Geringer. *Marriage on the Rocks.* New York: Delacorte, 1979.

Life-Stories

Allan, Chaney. *I'm Black and I'm Sober.* Minneapolis: CompCare, 1978.

Anderson, Louie. *Dear Dad: Letters From an Adult Child.* New York: Viking, 1989.

Caesar, Sid. *Where Have I Been?* New York: Signet Books, 1982.

Ford, Betty. *The Times of my Life.* New York: Ballantine Books, 1978.

DellaCorte, Betty. *Shelter From the Storm.* Glendale AZ: Villa Press, 1985.

Foster, Fred. *The Up and Outer.* Wheaton, IL: Tyndale House, 1980.

Howard, Marion. *Did I Have a Good Time?* New York: Continuum, 1981.

Hughes, Harold E. *The Man From Ida Grove.* Lincoln, VA: Chosen Books, 1979. (The Senator who persuaded the U.S. Government to fund alcoholism programs.)

Kirkpatrick, Jean. *Good-bye Hangovers, Hello Life.* New York: Atheneum, 1986. (Started "Women For Sobriety.")

Leite, Evelyn. *To Be Somebody.* Center City, MN: Hazelden, 1979.

Molloy, Paul. *Where Did Everybody Go?* Garden City, NY: Doubleday, 1981.

Marshall, Shelley. *Young, Sober and Free.* Center City, MN: Hazelden, 1978. (Stories of young people.)

Martin, Greg. *Spiritus Contra Spiritum.* Philadelphia: Westminster, 1977. (Struggle of an alcoholic pastor.)

Mehl, Duane. *At Peace With Failure.* Minneapolis: Augsburg, 1984. (A pastor's testimony of turning his life over to God.)

Newlove, Donald. *Those Drinking Days.* New York: Horizon Press, 1981.

Pinkham, Mary Ellen. *How to Stop the One You Love From Drinking.* New York: G. P. Putnam and Sons, 1986. (The author of "Mary Ellen's Help Hints" mentions her church connections positively.)

Rebeta-Burditt, Joyce. *The Cracker Factory.* New York: Macmillan, 1977.

Scoppettone, Sandra. *The Late Great Me.* New York: Bantam Books, 1976.

Somers, Suzanne. *Keeping Secrets.* New York: Warner Books, 1988. (Excellent on dilemma of adult children.)

Tamasi, Barbara. *I'll Stop Tomorrow.* Orleans, MA: Paraclete Press, 1982.

Wagner, Robin S., *Sarah T.—Portrait of a Teen-Age Alcoholic.* New York: Ballantine Books, 1975.

Whaley, Dennis (ed.). *Courage to Change.* Boston: Houghton-Mifflin, 1984. (Stories of 30 prominent persons who found sobriety.)

Church Ministry

Apthorp, Stephen P. *Alcohol and Substance Abuse—A Clergy Handbook.* Wilton, CT: Morehouse-Barlow, 1985.

Clinebell, Howard J. Jr. *Understanding and Counselling the Alcoholic.* Nashville, TN: Abingdon, 1978. (The basic book for pastors for counselling in regard to alcoholism.)

Come, Arnorld B. *Drinking: A Christian Position.* Philadelphia: Westminster Press, 1964.

Conley, Paul C. and Andrew A. Sorensen. *The Staggering Steeple.* Philadelphia: Pilgrim Press, 1971. (Order this historical book from North Conway Institute, 14 Beacon St. Boston, MA 02108.)

Fish, Melinda. *When Addiction Comes to Church.* Old Tappan, NJ: Chosen Books, 1990.

Keller, John. *Ministering to Alcoholics,* Minneapolis: Augsburg, 1966. (A standard, written before new genetic research.)

Marsh, Jack. *You Can Help the Alcoholic.* Notre Dame, IN: Ave Maria Press, 1983.

Morreim, Dennis. *Road to Recovery: Bridges Between the Bible and the Twelve Steps.* Minneapolis: Augsburg/ Fortress, 1990.

May, Gerald G. *Addiction and Grace.* New York: Harper & Row, 1988.

Nelson, James Douglas. *Awakening—Pastoring Health Through the Spiritual Principles of Shalom, Jesus and the Twelve Step Recovery Program.* Summit, PA: TAB Books, 1989.

Spickard, Anderson and Barbara R. Thompson. *Dying For A Drink.* Dallas, TX: Word, 1985. (Excellent gift book.)

Vaughn, Joe. *Family Intervention.* Louisville, KY: Westminster/John Knox, 1989.

Woodruff, C. Roy. *Alcoholism and Christian Experience.* Philadelphia: Westminster, 1968.

Bible Interpretation

Bouquet, A.C. *Everyday Life in New Testament Times.* New York: Charles Scribner and Sons, 1954.

Buttrick, George A. and Keith R. Crim. *Interpreter's Dictionary of the Bible.* Nashville, TN: Abingdon, 1971.

Charles, Howard H. *Alcohol and the Bible.* Scottdale, PA: Herald Press, 1966.

Douglas, J.D. (ed.). *Illustrated Bible Dictionary,* 3 Vols. Wheaton, IL: Tyndale House, 1980.

Gehman, Henry Snyder (ed.). *Westminster Dictionary of the Bible.* Philadelphia: Westminster, 1970.

Hewitt, T. Furman. *A Biblical Perspective on the Use of Alcohol and Other Drugs.* 1980. (Available from the Pastoral Care Council on Alcohol and Drug Abuse, Dept. of Human Resources, State of North Carolina. 325 N. Salisbury St., Raleigh, NC 27611.)

McKay, Alastair I. *Farming and Gardening in the Bible.* Emmaus, PA: Rodale Press, 1950.

Murphy, Richard T. A. *Background to the Bible.* Ann Arbor, MI: Servant Books, 1978.

Parker, J. I., et al. *The Bible Almanac.* Nashville, TN: Thomas Nelson, 1980.

Seltman, C. *Wine in the Ancient World.* London: Routledge, Kegan Paul, Ltd.: 1957.

Spahr, John Howard. *Sober Life.* Pittsburgh: Dorrance & Co., 1979.

Prevention

Holton, Helen T. *Proverbs For Prevention*. Dallas, TX: Tane Press, nd.

Luks, Allan. *Will America Sober Up?* Boston, MA: Beacon Press, 1983.

Manning, William O. and Jean Vinton. *Harmfully Involved*. Center City: Hazelden, 1978. (For School personnel and parents.)

Mosher, James F. *Prevention of Alcohol Problems*. nd. (Available from the Marin Institute for the Prevention of Alcohol and Other Problems, 1040 B St., Ste. 300, San Rafael, CA 94901.)

O'Gorman, Patricia. *Public Health Model of Prevention* [of alcohol problems]. Minneapolis: Johnson Institute, 1983.

Olson, Steve and Dean R. Gerstein. *Alcohol in America, Taking Action to Prevent Abuse*. Washington, DC: National Academy Press, 1985.

Pace, Nicholas A. *Guidelines to Safe Drinking*. New York: McGraw-Hill, 1984.

Wright, Roosevelt, Jr. and D. Watts (eds.). *Prevention of Black Alcoholism*. Springfield, IL: Charles C. Thomas, 1985.

Government and Legislation

Jacobson, Michael, Robert Atkins and George Hacker. *The Booze Merchants*. Washington, DC: Center for Science in the Public Interest, 1983.

McLennan, Ross J. *Booze, Bucks, Bamboozle and You*. Sane Press, 1978.

Mosher, James F. and Victor Colmon. *Alcoholic Beverage Control in a Public Health Perspective: A Handbook for Action*. 1989. Available from Marin Institute for the Prevention of Alcohol Problems, address above. (Based on the California situation but adaptable to other states.

Postman, N., et al. *Myths, Men and Beer—An Analysis of Beer Commercials on Broadcast TV in 1987*. (Available from the AAA Foundation for Traffic Safety, 2990 Telestar Court, Ste. 100, Falls Church, VA 22042.)

Weiner, Carolyn L. *Politics of Alcoholism*. New Brunswick, NJ: Transaction Books, 1981.

West, Louis Jolyon, (ed.). *Alcoholism and Related Problems—Issues for the American Public as Defined by the American Assembly—A Group of Prominent National Leaders*. Englewood Cliffs, NJ: Prentice-Hall, 1984.

Organization and Leadership

Flanagan, Joan. *The Successful Volunteer Organization*. Chicago, IL: Contemporary Books, 1981. (Available from Best Publications, 180 N. Michigan, Chicago, IL 60601.)

Kansas State University Extension Service. *A Key to Group Leadership*. Manhattan, KS: Kansas State University.

Roberts, Bruce B. and Howard I. Thorsheim. *Mutual Helping*. Northfield, MN: Social Ecology Resources, 1984. (Excellent treatise on how to get going on church or community projects. Available from P.O. Box 643, 55057.)

Wilson, Marlene. *How to Mobilize Church Volunteers*. Minneapolis: Augsburg, 1983.

2. Pamphlets

Alcohol and Alcoholism

About Alcohol; About Alcoholism; About Women and Alcohol; Alcohol on Campus. Channing L. Bete Co., Inc.

Alcohol and Aging. Alcohol Alert #2. NACADI, PH251.

The Alcoholism Complex—An Abstract of Dr. E. M. Jellinek's Book "The Disease Concept of Alcoholism". Christopher D. Smithers Foundation, 1965.

Alcohol and the Elderly, An Update. NACADI, MS306.

Alcoholism: A Merry-Go-Round Named Denial. Joseph L. Kellerman, Hazelden.

Alcoholism: The Needs of Minorities. Fred T. Davis, Jr. NCA, 1973.

Almost All You Wanted to Know About Alcoholism. Robert L. Hammond, 1986 (available from Hazelden).

Don't Panic, Here Are 12 Reasons Why You Can't Be An

Alcoholic. Robert L. Hammond, ARIS, 1987.

The Fact Is . . . Resources Are Available on Alcohol and Other Drugs and the Disabled Person. (Extensive list of programs, organizations and published materials.) #MS339 NACADI.

The Gay Drinking Problem. John Michael. CompCare.

Genetic and Environmental Factors Leading to Alcoholism. C. Robert Cloninger. Johnson Institute, 1983.

I Can't Be An Alcoholic Because. David C. Hancock, Hazelden. (Also in Spanish.)

If You Drink, What You Should Know and Do. Hazelden.

Learn About Series. Hazelden, 1983 ff. (13 pamphlets on various aspects of alcohol and other drug abuse.)

Plight of the Elderly Alcoholic. NCA, 1981. (Available from NACADI, RPO/469.)

Some Medical Aspects of Alcohol and Other Drug Abuse; Alcohol and Nutrition; Alcohol and Diabetes; Sexuality, Alcohol and Drugs. Dr. Max Schneider. (Available from NCA.)

What Every Teen-Ager Should Know About Alcohol. Channing L. Bete, Inc.

What is Alcohol and Why Do People Drink? Center for Alcohol Studies, Rutgers University, 1976.

Treatment and Recovery

About AA—Newsletter for Professionals. AA General Services.

About Alcohol Services. Channing L. Bete Co., Inc.

Black, Beautiful and Recovering. Gloria McGee, et al. Hazelden.

Chemical-Dependency and the African-American. Peter Bell. Hazelden.

Counseling Ethnic Minorities. Jerry Spicer. Hazelden.

The Deadly Silence: Friendship and Drinking Problems. Jon R. Weinberg. Hazelden.

The Dry Drunk Syndrome. R.J. Solberg. Hazelden.

The Dry Drunk Revisited. R.J. Solberg. Hazelden.

The Elderly, A Guide for Counsellors. Bobby Walker and Phil Kelly. Hazelden.

Gay and Lesbian Alcoholics, AA's Message of Hope. Hazelden.

Going Home, A Re-entry Guide for the Newly Sober. Janet Geringer Woititz. CompCare.

Grief, A Basic Reaction to Alcoholism. Joseph Kellerman. Hazelden.

Intervention. Freedom Institute, 1980. (Available from NCA.)

The Kemper Approach to Alcoholism, Drug Addiction and Other Living Problems. Frederick Willman et al. Kemper Insurance Group.

Lesbian and Gay Issues in Early Recovery. Renee Gosselin. Hazelden.

The Psychopathology of Denial. Daniel J. Anderson. Hazelden.

Sexuality and Recovery. Barbara McFarland. Hazelden, 1984.

Sober Days, Golden Years. Johnson Institute, 1982.

Surrender versus Compliance in Therapy. Harry M. Tiebout. NCA, 1953.

Twelve Step Pamphlets. various authors. Hazelden.

Women's Powerlessness. Janice N. Hazelden, 1985.

Women and Relapse. Suzanne Boylston Cusack. Hazelden, 1984.

Children and Family

Al-Anon, You and the Alcoholic. Al-Anon Family Groups. (Explains Al-Anon.)

The Al-Anon Focus. Al-Anon Family Groups. (For recovering alcoholics affected by problem drinking of others.)

Al-Anon is for Adult Children of Alcoholics. Al-Anon Family Groups.

Alcoholism in the Family. Channing L. Bete Co., Inc.

But I Didn't Make Any Noise About It. Cindy Lewis-Steere. CompCare.

Children of Alcoholics. Roy W. Pickens. Hazelden.

Counseling the Alcoholic and the Family. Yvelin Gardner, NCA, 1970.

Depression and Alcoholism. Dorothy Hatsukami and Roy

Pickens. Hazelden.

Drinking and Pregnancy. Johnston Institute, 1981.

The Fact Is . . . Alcohol and Other Drugs Can Harm an Unborn Baby. 1981, NACADI, #MS353.

Guide for the Family of the Alcoholic. Joseph L. Kellerman. Hazelden, 1977.

Guide to the Fourth Step Inventory for the Spouse. Hazelden.

If Your Parents Drink Too Much. Al-Anon Family Groups. 1974. (Cartoon booklet.)

Points for Parents Perplexed About Drugs. David C. Hancock. Hazelden.

Teen-agers Speak For Abstinence. Preferred Risk Insurance Co.

Women and Alcohol. NACADI. #RPO716.

Prevention

Alcoholism—How Can We Help Prevent It? Contact Magazine, #92. (Available from Christian Medical Commission of the World Council of Churches, 475 Riverside Dr., #1062, New York, NY 10115. One of the few articles dealing with alcohol problems worldwide.)

Choosing Not to Drink. Channing L. Bete Co., Inc.

Crossing the Thin Line Between Social Drinking and Alcoholism. Terrence Williams. Hazelden.

If You are a Professional, AA Wants to Work with You. AA World Services, Inc., 1972.

It's All Right to Say: "Thanks I Don't Drink". Christopher D. Smithers Foundation.

Our Approach to Alcoholism: A Shift in Paradigm is Not Necessary. John Wallace. Johnson Institute, 1984.

Personal Responsible Abstinence. North Conway Institute.

Preventing Alcoholism. Christopher D. Smithers Foundation, 1978.

Primary Prevention is Possible. David C. Hancock. (Available from same: 4616 Longfellow Ave. So., Minneapolis, MN 55407.)

The Public Health Model of Prevention. Patricia O'Gorman. Johnson Institute, 1983.

Stopping Alcohol and Other Drug Abuse Before It Starts: The Future of Prevention. Office For Substance Abuse Prevention (OSAP) Prevention Monograph-1. NACADI, BK160.

Tools For Prevention, Women and Alcohol Problems. NACADI, PH220.

Church Ministry

Alcohol, Alcoholism and Social Drinking: Statement of the Joint Commission on Alcoholism of the Protestant Episcopal Church in the U.S.A. Seabury Press, 1958, 1979.

Alcoholism, Drug Abuse and the Church—A Call To Action. (Available from The Church Pension Fund, 800 2nd Ave., New York, NY 10017. A plan for implementing the 1979 Resolution of the Episcopal Church.)

Alcohol Use and Abuse: The Social and Health Effects. Reports and Recommendations by the Presbyterian Church (U.S.A.). 1986. (Available from Presbyterian Distribution Management Services, 1-800-524-2612. Louisville, KY.)

Alcohol-Drug Awareness Resources. Presbyterian Church (U.S.A.) and Presbyterian Network on Alcohol and Other Drug Abuse, 1988-90. (Available same as above.)

Christian Ministry and the Fifth Step. Edward C. Sellner. Hazelden, 1981.

The Church and Alcohol. David C. Hancock. (Address given at the International Conference of Religious Leaders on the Impact of Alcohol and Other Drugs on Contemporary Society, Indianapolis, IN, 1979. Order from Hancock address under Prevention.)

Confronting Alcohol Problems In Your Congregation. Bob H. Adams. CompCare, 1983.

Drug and Alcohol Concerns. General Conference of the United Methodist Church Statements, (CS91). (Available from Discipleship Resources, P.O. Box 189, Nashville, TN 37202.)

God Help Me to be Me: Spiritual Growth During Recovery. Vernon E. Johnson. Johnson Institute, 1991.

How to Produce a Clergy Workshop. Michael L. Schmidt. NCA 1983.

Pastoral Counseling and the Alcoholic. E. A. Verdrey. NCA, 1986.

Recovery from the Disease of Alcoholism: Role of the Clergy. Clergy Committee of the Alcoholism Council of Cincinnati, 125 William Taft Road, Cincinnati, OH 45219.

Stumbling Blocks or Stepping Stones. Karl A. Schneider. (Address given to National Council on Alcoholism Forum, San Diego, CA, 1977. NCA)

Miscellaneous

Guidelines for Support Groups. Janet G. Woititz. Health Communications, 1986.

Organizing a Volunteer Program. Larry Winecoff and Conrad Powell. Pendell Publishing Co.

The Spiritual Progression Chart. James E. Royce. Hazelden.

Tainted Booze. Charles P. Mitchell and Michael F. Jacobson. Washington, DC: Center for Science in the Public Interest, 1987.

Truth For Youth Poster Set. Pasadena Council on Alcoholism, P.O. Box 60934, Pasadena, CA 91106. (Excellent series using pictures and testimonies of famous athletes.)

Women and the Abuse of Prescription Drugs. Myron Brenton. Public Affairs Pamphlets, New York.

3. Videos, Films, Audiocassettes

Videos are replacing films at a rapid rate, both as new productions and reproductions of former films. They both are sold or rented by many publishers who specialize in educational materials regarding alcohol and drug problems (e.g. CompCare, Hazelden, Health Communications, Johnston Institute and Parkside). Their addresses are in the publishers section, (#6). Audio cassettes are available from the same sources.

Because videos and films are expensive, you might inquire at your local branch of the National Council on Alcoholism, at nearby treatment programs, schools or denominational resource offices whether you can borrow from their collection. Doing so has the added advantage of being able to preview them easily as well as to get some idea from the lending organization as to their usefulness. These same locales are apt to have audio cassettes also, although they are relatively inexpensive to buy.

Following are five additional sources which specialize in these helps:

Addiction Counselor's Continuing Education Services, Inc., P.O. Box 30380, Indianapolis, IN 46230.
AIMS Instructional Media, Inc. 626 Justin Ave., Glendale, CA 91201.
Narcotics Education, Inc., 6830 Laurel St. NW, Washington, DC 20012-9979.
NCADI. Maintains a collection of video tapes that may be borrowed at no cost. P.O. Box 2345, Rockville, MD 20904
PYRAMID–85, Film and Video, Box 1048, Santa Monica, CA 90406.

There are many excellent videos and films available, but the following four are outstanding in dealing with their particular subjects:

A Gift of Life. American Council for Drug Education, 204 Monroe St., Rockville, MD 20850. (Youth oriented.)
The Honour of All. Phil Lucas Productions. Available from Hazelden. (A three part series telling the story of the heroic struggle of the Alkali Indian tribe in British Columbia to overcome widespread alcoholism. Inspiring and instructive.)
Is There an Elephant in Your Sanctuary? (A unique challenge to the local congregation to get into alcohol ministry.) Order from David L. Zuverink, Presbyterian Church, U.S.A., 100 Witherspoon St., Room 3060, Louisville, KY 40202-1396.
Social Model Approach to Recovery. Burbank, CA: Bridge Focus, 1990. (A singular five-part study of the social-model approach. Goes with the book of the same title.)

❧ ❧ ❧ ❧

Drama is an effective way to present problematical subjects—especially for young people. Following is an excellent source:

Plays for Living. Family Service Association of America, 44 East 23rd St., New York, NY 10010.

4. Curricula

Adult

The Church and Alcohol. Rev. A. Philip Parham and Patricia Merrill, 1983. (St. Paul's Episcopal Church) San Antonio Council on Alcoholism, 5307 Broadway, Ste. 226, San Antonio, TX 78209. (Good background material, includes study outlines and handouts for copying.)

The Church and Chemical Health. Synod of the Lakes and Prairies, 1983. Presbyterian Church, (U.S.A.), 8012 Cedar Ave. So., Bloomington, MN 5540. (Comprehensive resource manual oriented toward adults with workshop plans and basic information.)

Christ in the Vineyard. Summit Publications, 1982. Box 204, La Cañada, CA 91101. (Attractive course of eight sessions with tapes and explanatory material.)

The Religious Community and Mental Health. Minnesota Prevention Resource Center, 2829 Verndale Ave., Anoka, MN 55303. (An interfaith guide to alcohol and drug use issues intended to help develop an effective response to chemical use problems.)

Children and Youth

An Elephant in the Living Room. Jill M. Hastings and Marion H. Typpo. CompCare. (For children 7 years through early adolescence. Leaders' guide available.)

BABES (Beginning Alcohol and Addictions Basic Education Studies). NCA/NARCO-Greater Detroit Area, 1800 Kales Building, 76 W. Adams, Detroit, MI 48226. (An outstanding program for very young children who live in alcoholic homes. Leadership training.)

Born Free, Stay Free. A drug prevention program of the South Carolina United Methodist Church. Dick Gibson, 150 St. John's Court, Rock Hill, SC 29730. (Includes parents and children [grades 1 to 12] in joint and separate sessions. Leadership training events.)

D.A.V.I.D. Milford Presbyterian Church, 238 N. Main St., Milford, MI 48042. (Video and leaders' guide and participant packet to help plan an alcohol/drug abuse workshop.)

8:30 Monday Morning. ARIS. (Comprehensive, attractive material for grades 7 through 12.)

Facts, Feelings, Family and Friends. Linda Christensen. Johnson Institute, 1990. (Twenty easy-to-use lesson plans for kindergarten through sixth grade.)

Free to Know, Free to Choose. Prepared by Chemical Use Task Force of the Lutheran Church of America, Minnesota Synod. Harper/Hazelden. (Four sessions for use with 12- to 15-year-olds in church school or other religious education settings.)

From Peer Pressure to Peer Support. Johnson Institute, 1990. (Prevention through group process for grades 7 through 12. Emphasizes parent and school cooperation.)

You, Your Body and Alcohol. Evelyn and Bob Hickle and Linda Jane Vogel. General Board of Church and Society of the United Methodist Church. (For older elementary students in the church school.)

5. Magazines and Newsletters

Alcohol Health and Research World. National Institute on Alcohol Abuse and Alcoholism. Quarterly. (Subscriptions or single copies available from Superintendent of Documents. Excellent source of up-to-date information.)

Bottom Line. ARIS. Quarterly. (Correlated up-to-date information in very readable form.)

Monday Morning Report. ARIS. Newsletter published twice monthly.

DAC Bulletin. General Board of Church and Society of the

United Methodist Church. (Information of special interest to churches.)

Journal of Studies on Alcohol. Quarterly. Rutgers Center of Alcohol Studies. (Very prestigious in the field.)

LISTEN. Monthly. 12501 Old Columbia Pike, Silver Spring, MD 20904-6600. (Attractive, for young people.)

Prevention Pipeline. Office of Substance Abuse for the Alcohol (OSAP), Drug Abuse and Mental Health Administration. (Available from NACADI. Latest developments on prevention front sharing information on programs and timely publications.)

U.S. Journal of Drug and Alcohol Dependence. Monthly. (Trade paper for addictions professionals. Also publishes *Changes* for adult children of alcoholics; and *Focus* for family addictions specialists. Not a government entity.)

6. Publishers and Other Sources for Publications and Helps

These publishers, distributors and sellers specialize in publications on alcohol and other drug abuse. All will be glad to send their catalogs upon request. Books from general publishers may be ordered through local bookstores. (See listings under Organizations, also.)

Addiction Research Foundation of Ontario. 33 Russell St., Toronto, Ontario, Canada M5S 251.

Alcohol Research Library. 1816 Scenic Ave., Berkeley, CA 94709.

ARIS (Alcohol Research Information Service). 1106 E. Oakland Ave., Lansing, MI 48906.

Channing L. Bete Co., Inc. 200 State Rd., South Deerfield, MA 01373.

Bridge Focus. 2829 N. Glenoaks, #206, Burbank, CA 91504.

Catbird Seat Bookstore. 913 SW Broadway, Portland, OR 97205.

Center for Science in the Public Interest (CSPI). 1501 16th St., Washington, DC 20036.

CompCare. 2415 Annapolis Lane, Minneapolis, MN 55441.

Daughters of St. Paul. 50 St. Paul's Ave., Boston, MA

02130.

Hazelden. Box 176, Center City, MN 55012-0176.

Health Communications, Inc. Enterprise Center, 3201 SW 15th St., Deerfield Beach, FL 33442-8124.

Johnson Institute. 7151 Metro Blvd., Minneapolis, MN 55439-2122.

Kemper Group. (Insurance Companies) Public Requests Desk, Corporate Relations Dept F-6, Kemper Groups, Long Grove, IL 60049.

Military Family Resource Center. Ballston Towers, #3, Suite 903, 4015 Wilson Blvd., Arlington, VA 22203.

NACADI (National Clearinghouse for Alcohol and Drug Information [Federal Government]) P.O. Box 2345, Rockville, MD 20852.

Narcotics Education, Inc. P.O. Box 10548 Silver Springs, MD 20904-0548.

NCA (National Council on Alcoholism). 12 W. 21st St., New York, NY 10010.

Parkside Publishing Corporation. 205 W. Touhy Ave., Park Ridge, IL 60068.

Perrin and Treggett, Booksellers. P.O. Box 190, Rutherford, NJ 07070.

Preferred Risk Insurance Companies. 1111 Ashworth Road, West Des Moines, IA 50265.

Public Affairs Pamphlets. 381 Park Ave. South, New York, NY 10016.

Rutgers Center on Alcohol Studies. Publications Division, P.O. Box 969, Piscataway, NJ 08854.

The Christopher D. Smithers Foundation, Inc. Box 67, Mill Neck, NY 11765.

Spenco. Box 8113, Waco, TX 76710.

Southern Baptist Convention, The Christian Life Commission. 460 James Robertson Parkway, Nashville, TN 37219.

Tane Press. 6778 Greenville, Dallas, TX 75231.

United Methodist Church, General Board of Church and Society. 1908 Grand Ave. P.O. Box 189, Nashville, TN 37202.

University of Michigan Press. Box 1104, Ann Arbor, MI 48106.

U.S. Journal, Inc. Enterprise Center, 3201 SW 15th St., Deerfield Beach, FL 33442-8124. (Not a government entity.)

U.S. Superintendent of Documents. U.S. Government Printing Office, Washington, DC 20402.

Wisconsin Clearinghouse. P.O. Box 1468, Madison, WI 53701.

7. Organizations

Many of these organizations have literature and other helps available.

Al-Anon Adult Children's Groups. Al-Anon Family Group Headquarters, Inc., Dept P1/C, P.O. Box 862, Midtown Station, New York, NY 10018.

Al-Anon Family Group Headquarters. P.O. Box 182, Madison Square Station, New York, NY 10159-0182. (Local groups listed in telephone Yellow Pages.)

Alcohol and Drug Abuse Committee of the Presbytery of Detroit. 17575 Hubbell, Detroit, MI 48235-2797.

Alcohol and Drug Problems Association of North America. 1101-15th St. NW, Washington, DC 20005.

Alcoholics Anonymous World Services. Box 459, Grand Central Station, New York, NY 10116. (Local groups listed in Yellow Pages.)

Alcoholics Victorious. 123 S. Green St., Chicago, IL 60007.

American Council on Alcoholism. 300 E. Joppa Rd., Suite 168, Baltimore, MD 21204. (Not to be confused with American Council on Alcohol Problems.)

American Council on Alcohol Problems (ACAP). 3426 Bridgeland Dr., Bridgeton, MO 63044-2695. (Will give the address of related state organizations.)

American Council for Drug Education. 204 Monroe St., Rockville, MD 203850.

American Indians for Sobriety (AIS). P.O. Box 372. Moapa, NV 89025.

Association of Halfway House Alcoholism Programs of North America. 786 E. 7th St., St. Paul, MN 55106.

BACCHUS. P.O. Box 10430, Denver, CO 80210. (On college and university campuses.)

Children of Alcoholics Foundation. 200 Park Ave., 31st Floor, New York, NY 10166.

The Congress on Chemical Dependency and Disability. 15519 Crenshaw Blvd., Suite 209, Gardena, CA 90249.

Families Anonymous. P.O. Box 528, Van Nuys, CA 91408.

Impaired Physician's Program. 5775 Peachtree—Dunwoody Road, Atlanta, GA 30342.

International Advisory Council for Homosexual Men and Women in A.A. P.O. Box 90, Washington, DC 20041.

Jaycees (U.S. Junior Chamber of Commerce). P.O. Box 7, Tulsa, OK 74121.

MADD (Mothers Against Drunk Driving). 669 Airport Freeway, Hurst, TX 76053.

Manhattan Bowery Association. 275 Seventh Ave., New York, NY 10001.

Michigan Communities in Action for Drug Free Youth. 470 N. Woodward Ave., Birmingham, MI 48011.

NACOA (National Association for Children of Alcoholics). 31582 Coast Highway, Suite B., South Laguna, CA 92677-3044.

National Association of Gay Alcoholism Counselors. 204 W. 20th St., New York, NY 10011.

National Black Alcoholism Council. 53 W. Jackson, #828, Chicago, IL 60604.

National Catholic Council on Alcoholism. 1200 Varnum St. NE, Washington, DC 20017-2796. (Originally clergy but now open to lay persons also, Catholic or Protestant.)

National Coalition of Hispanic Mental Health and Human Services Organizations. 1010-15th St. NW, Suite 402, Washington, DC 20005.

National Episcopal Coalition on Alcohol and Drugs. 1511 K St. NW, Suite 715, Washington, DC 20005.

National Federation of Parents for Drug-Free Youth. 1423 N. Jefferson, Springfield, MO 65802. (Sponsors Red-Ribbon Week.)

National Indian Board on Alcohol and Drug Abuse. P.O. Box 8, Turtle Lake, WI 54889.

National P.T.A. Alcohol and Drug Project. 700 N. Rush St.

Chicago, IL 60611.

National Safety Council. 444 N. Michigan Ave., Chicago, IL 60611.

North Conway Institute. 14 Beacon St., Boston, MA 02108. (Pioneer in alcoholism prevention programs by the religious community.)

Overcomers Outreach. Bob and Pauline Bartosch, 2290 W. Whittier Blvd., Suite 8-D, La Habra, CA 90631. (Relates 12 Steps to Scriptures.)

Palmer Drug Abuse Program (PDAP). P.O. Box 460, Milford, MI 48042. (Church related program for youth and their parents.)

Parent Support Group, Inc. P.O. Box 503, Glen Park, NJ 07452.

Phoenix House Foundation. 164 W. 74th St., New York, NY 10023.

Presbyterian Network on Alcohol and Other Drug Abuse (PNAODA). PHEWA, 3B-3041 Presbyterian Center, 100 Witherspoon St., Louisville, KY 40202-1396.

Prevention of Alcohol Problems, Inc. 4616 Longfellow Ave. So., Minneapolis, MN 55407. (Provides religious community at all levels with education through seminars, speakers, evaluation and research.)

PRIDE (National Parents Resource Institute for Drug Education). 100 Edgewood Ave., Suite 1002, Atlanta, GA 30303.

Prison Fellowship International. P.O. Box 17434, Washington, DC 20041. (Started by Charles Colson. Includes alcoholism groups.)

RACA (Recovered Alcoholic Clergy Association). c/o St. Boniface Church, 5615 Midnightpost Rd., Sarasota, FL 34242. (Chiefly Episcopal.)

RID. P.O. Box 520, Schenectady, NY 12301. (Educates about drunk-driving laws, convictions, etc.)

SADD (Students Against Driving Drunk). P.O. Box 800, Marlboro, MA 01752.

Salvation Army. 799 Bloomfield Ave., Verona, NJ 07044.

Shepherd's Fold Ministries. 1324 El Rancho Dr., Santa Cruz, CA 95060. (Involves street people.)

SOAR (Society of Americans for Recovery, Inc.). 600 E. 14th

St., Des Moines, IA 50316. (Started in 1990 by Senator Harold Hughes to combat discrimination against recovering persons because of financial, social, legal or health care problems.)

Teen Challenge. 1525 N. Campbell Ave., Springfield, MO 65803. (Associated with General Council of the Assemblies of God.)

Toughlove. P.O. Box 70, Sellersville, PA 18960. (Parents support group.)

Trauma Foundation. Building One, Room 306, San Francisco General Hospital, San Francisco, CA 94110. (Specializes in legal matters.)

Volunteers of America. 3813 N. Causeway Blvd., Metairie, LA 70002.

Women for Sobriety. P.O. Box 618, Quakertown, PA 18951. (Recovery groups for women. Very good literature.)

❧ ❧ ❧ ❧

State Governmental Offices. All states and territories have offices for alcohol and other drug concerns. Write to the state or territorial capital for name and address.

8. Outstanding Programs

These are church related programs who will gladly share their experiences.

Alcohol Consultation Services (ACS). Westminster Presbyterian Church, 724 Delaware Ave., Buffalo, NY 14209. (Assists members of the congregation to find help for their own or family members' alcohol problems.)

Alcohol and Drug Ministries. Rev. Robert D. McNeil, Ecumenical Ministries of Oregon, 0245 SW Bancroft St., Portland, OR 97201. (Especially interested in training of pastors.)

Alcohol Services of San Diego—Public Inebriety Intervention, P.O. Box 85222, San Diego, CA 92138-5222. (An effective plan to deal with public drunkenness.)

Atlanta Professional Alliance. MARR (Metro Atlanta Recovery Residences) P.O. Box 1385, Clarkston, GA 30021. (Offers extended specialized programs.)

Born Free, Stay Free. Dick Gibson, Director, 150 St. John's Court, Rock Hill, SC 29730. (A drug prevention program for youth by the South Carolina United Methodist Conference. See also under Curricula.)

Christ in the Vineyard. La Cañada Presbyterian Church, P.O. Box 188, La Cañada, CA 91011. (A Christian 11th Step group.)

Community Advisory Committee on Aging and Addiction. Eleanore Schafer, Top-o'the-Hill-Gang, St. Lukes Behavioral Health Center, 1800 E. Van Buren, Phoenix, AZ 85006.

Cottage Meeting Program. 736 S. 500 East, Salt Lake City, UT 84102. (A neighborhood outreach program with meetings held by interested persons in homes, clubs, churches, etc. Training opportunities provided.)

Faith House. 4506 W. Citrus Way, Glendale, AZ 85301. (A crisis shelter for families of alcoholics with programs—residential and outpatient—for all ages. See: *Shelter From the Storm,* by Betty DellaCorte under "Life Stories".)

Family Center. Rev. Roger M. Smith, Roslyn Presbyterian Church, Roslyn, NY 11576. (Outstanding program for all family members. Includes training for clergy.)

Logos House. Barry McCabe, 802 N. 2nd, Tacoma, WA 98403. (Well-rounded, growing program related to the Assembly of God Church.)

Metro Atlanta Recovery Residences, Inc. (MARR). Rev. Mike Gibson, P.O. Box 85, Clarkston, GA 30021. (Each residence relates to a local church where spiritual-life groups are held.)

National Capital Presbytery Health Ministries. 4915 - 45th St. NW, Washington, DC 20016-2790. (Includes alcoholism program.)

New Beginnings. First Presbyterian Church, 4815 Franklin Road, Nashville, TN 37220. (Promoted by Dr. Anderson Spickard, co-author of *Dying for a Drink.* See Books / Church Ministry.)

New Directions. P.O. Box 1911, Brentwood, TN 37027.

(Home Bible study consisting of four workbooks relating to recovery.)

The Overcomers. Calvary Chapel, 367 Mt. Paran Rd. NW, Atlanta, GA 30327. (Emphasizes God and Christ as "Higher Power".)

Presbyterian Alcohol and Drug Alliance. PAADA, 1550 W. Edgemont, Phoenix, AZ 85007. (Aegis of Presbytery of Grand Canyon. An effective regional program.)

Palavra Tree. Rev. Cleo Malone, 1212 S. 43rd St., #D, San Diego, CA 92113. (Intense alcohol program which is part of a larger neighborhood program for Afro-American residents. Strong church emphasis.)

The Peer Counseling Book. Carol Hacker, 200 S. Marshall, Lakewood, CO 80226. (A training program for high school counselors.)

Powell III Chemical Dependency Center. Iowa Methodist Medical Center, 2023 Grand Ave., Des Moines, IA 50312. (Conducts Children's Feelings Groups while parents are in treatment.)

Project DARE. (Drug and Alcohol Resources for the Elderly), 3535 SW Kelly, Portland, OR 97201. (Sponsored by the Ecumenical Ministries of Oregon.)

Turning Point of Central California. 119 S. Locust, Visalia, CA 93291. (Educates and treats all ages having drug and alcohol problems. Outstanding example of a program organized by a consortium of eight churches to meet a community need. Now free-standing.)

Westminster Presbyterian Church Chemical Dependency Awareness Committee. Nicollet Mall at 12th St., Minneapolis, MN 55403. (Excellent materials.)

XYZ Project. Downtown United Presbyterian Church, 121 N. Fitzhugh St., Rochester, NY 14614. (For young people who are in treatment for substance abuse or are returning from treatment centers.)

9. Training

These training opportunities have been selected because of their quality and scope of courses both for lay and professional people. Many of them offer studies related to religion and spirituality in regard to alcohol problems.

Annual Conference of Canadian Federation on Alcohol and Drug Dependencies. Addiction Research Foundation of Ontario, 33 Russell St., Toronto, Ontario, Canada M5S 2S1.

Berkeley Center for Alcohol Studies. 1798 Scenic Ave., Berkeley, CA 94709.

Eastern Pennsylvania Institute of Alcohol Studies. 2101 N. Front St., Riverside Bldg. #1, Harrisburg, PA 17110.

International School of Alcohol Studies. Div. of Alcoholism/ Drug Abuse, 320 Avenue B, East, Bismarck, ND 58505.

Johnson Institute. 7151 Metro Blvd., Minneapolis, MN 55439-2122.

Hazelden Foundation. Box 176, Center City, MN 55012-0176.

New York State Alcohol Institutes, Division of Alcoholism. 44 Holland Ave., Albany, NY 12229.

Oregon Institute of Addiction Studies. P.O. Box 7373, Salem, OR 97303.

Preferred Risk Insurance Companies. 1111 Ashworth Rd., West Des Moines, IA 50265. (Clergy training workshops.)

Prevention of Alcohol Problems, Inc. Rev. David C. Hancock, 4616 Longfellow Ave. So., Minneapolis, MN 55407.

Rutgers Summer School of Alcohol Studies. Smithers Hall, New Brunswick, NJ 08903.

Seattle University Alcohol Studies Program. Seattle, WA 98122.

South Carolina School of Alcohol and Drug Studies. P.O. Box 4616, Columbia, SC 29240.

Texas Institute of Alcohol Studies. Texas Commission on Alcoholism, 809 Sam Houston State Office Bldg., Austin, TX 78701.

University of Utah School on Alcoholism and Other Drug Abuse. P.O. Box 2604, Salt Lake City, UT 84110.

U.S. Journal Training, Inc. Enterprise Center, 3201 SW 15th St., Deerfield Beach, FL 33442-8124. (Offers workshops throughout U.S.)

10. Seminaries

The following theological seminaries offer courses in ministry with alcohol problems. Often they will share their experience and curricula information with other seminaries or pastoral training schools. See also p. 161 of text.

Andover-Newton Theological School, 210 Herrick Rd., Newton Center, MA 02159.

Austin Presbyterian Theological School, 100 E. 27th St., Austin, TX 78705

Charles Cook Theological School, 708 Lindon Lane, Tempe, AZ 85281. (Offers an outstanding curricula in dealing with Native American milieu.)

Christian Theological Seminary, 1000 W. 42nd St., Indianapolis, IN 46208.

Columbia Theological Seminary, 701 Columbia Dr., Box 520, Decatur, GA 30031.

Episcopal Divinity School, 90 Brattle St., Cambridge, MA 02138.

Fuller Theological Seminary, 135 N. Oakland, Pasadena, CA 91101-1790.

Graduate Theological Union Cooperative, 1798 Scenic Ave., Berkeley, CA 94709.

Jewish Theological Seminary of America, 3080 Broadway, New York, NY 10027.

Lutheran Theological Southern Seminary, 4201 N. Main, Columbia, SC 29203.

Mennonite Brethren Biblical Seminary, 4824 E. Butler, Fresno, CA 93727.

Pacific Lutheran Theological Seminary, 2770 Marin Ave., Berkeley, CA 94708.

Pittsburgh Theological Seminary, 616 N. Highland Ave., Pittsburgh, PA 15206.

Union Theological Seminary in Virginia, 3401 Brook Rd., Richmond, VA 23227.

University of Dubuque Theological Seminary, 2000 University Ave., Dubuque, IA 52001. (Has well-developed curriculum outlines.)

11. Suggestions For Worship

A Celebration in Worship (A Service)

Prelude

Call to Worship
Silent Preparation
Congregation: "The Spirit of the Lord is upon us, because the Lord has anointed us to bring good news to the afflicted; he has sent us to bind up the broken-hearted, to proclaim liberty to the captives and the opening of the prison to those who are bound (from Is 61:1).
Leader: Your eye is upon us, O God; you see our going out and our coming in. You know when we gather in praise of your name. You are aware of our needs, how we yearn for peace in our souls. You are compassionate and tender, embracing us with your love. Hear us in our whispering and listen to our loud praise as we honor you this day.

Hymn: "Praise To the Lord"

Prayer of Confession (In unison): Our Father, forgive us when we have been insensitive to the cries for help from our fellow men and women. Have mercy upon us when we have been too busy to become involved in the hurts of our brothers and sisters who have been afflicted with alcoholism. We regret that our church has not done more to bring hope and healing to not only alcoholics, but also to their families in the midst of their suffering and to others injured in body and spirit because of someone's thoughtless imbibing. Father, as you sent your Son to us "to set the prisoners free", set us free to minister to and with those afflicted by the misuse of alcohol, acclaiming the Good News of our freedom through Jesus Christ our Lord. Amen.

Silent, Personal Confession

Assurance of Pardon (In unison): The saying is sure and worthy of full acceptance, that Christ Jesus came into the world to save sinners. Therefore, if any one is in Christ, he is a new creation; the old has passed away, behold, the new has come. The mercy of the Lord is from everlasting to everlasting, therefore, in the name of Jesus Christ we are forgiven.

Hymn: "Amazing Grace"

Experiences of Grace: (Testimonies of a few recovering persons—an alcoholic, a child, spouse, parent or sibling of an alcoholic.)
Sermon

Fellowship of Prayer: (Requests and prayers from the congregation.)

Hymn: "We Give Thee But Thine Own"

Benediction

Liturgical suggestions

Scriptures:

Isaiah 61:1; Luke 4:16-21; Luke 15:11-24; Acts 2:42-47; Romans 7:24-25; Galatians 5:13-25; Galatians 6:1-10; Ephesians 3:16-19 and Ephesians 6:1-20.

Hymns:

- "Lonely Voices in the City"
- "There Is a Balm in Gilead"
- "Make Me a Captive, Lord"
- "There's a Wideness in God's Mercy"
- "O the Deep, Deep Love of Jesus"
- "Amazing Grace"

Sermon Subjects:

- The Church's Ministry to Alcoholics
- What the Church can Learn from AA
- Setting the Prisoners Free
- From Tragedy to Triumph
- The Agony and the Ecstasy
  See also: Five Sermon Outlines in *Alcohol and Substance Abuse,* by Stephen P. Apthorp, Wilton, CT, Morehouse-Barlow, 1985.

Prayers:

- We pray for our Task Force on alcohol problems that your holy presence may enter deeply into our dreams and visions. Persevere with us who are so small and weak alongside of the alcohol problems in our world. Do not abandon us. Give us joy in our work and singing in our hearts and ever-renewed strength for our task and love for each other. Amen.
- A *"Third-Step" Prayer*—God, I offer myself to Thee—to build with me and to do with me as Thou wilt. Relieve me of the bondage of self that I may better do Thy will. Take away my difficulties that victory over them may bear witness to those I would help. May I do Thy will always! Amen.
- A *Prayer for Alcoholics*—God our Father, to all who have begun the pilgrimage to a better world and whose hearts are homeless in this one, grant your grace that they may be strengthened in their journey. And if by chance they should come close to us in their travels, give us the sensitivity to open wide the doors of our lives and greet them: "Welcome sister or brother! Come in and rest awhile." Grant most merciful God, to all who travel the by-ways of this world looking for freedom and adventure and love, a peace beyond all their anguish. Strengthen them and us for deeds and dreams that shall outlast all our fears and doubts and bring us at last through the gates of

heaven into your everlasting presence. Amen.

A Litany of Concern:

Pastor: Jesus, you are the Servant example to us. You ministered to the alienated—the afflicted with bodily, mental and moral disease. You offered them the healing power of Your Servant Love.

People: We are your people. Help us to minister as you have ministered to our needs. May we likewise reach out to the outcasts of our age and our community.

Pastor: Help us, Lord, to lift the lazy lids of our eyes to see those suffering from addictions.

People: We confess that the stigmatizing of the "junkie" and the "alcoholic" as the "skid row bum" has kept us from offering ourselves. We have conveniently overlooked learning the facts of addiction. Quietly we have ignored our own compulsive habits of eating, overworking and smoking.

Pastor: Help us as God's people and concerned citizens.

People: Help us provide adequate treatment and rehabilitation opportunities to help the addicted become liberated.

Pastor: Lord, we would ask your grace to make us whole.

People: Help us to share your healing power by just laws and cooperation with voluntary and governmental agencies in a total involvement of the community.

Pastor: Your love presents us with new opportunities.

People: We would grow and become responsible servants to our congregation, our community, the addicted and their families and to each other as persons of concern.

Pastor: As we experience your Sonship anew, may we include all alienated—the aged, the youth, the sick and the sorrowful in your steadfast love.

People: Amen.

(These liturgical suggestions [except for the reference to Dr. Arthorp's sermon outlines] have been gleaned from sometime papers by Rev. C. Howard Wallace and Rev. Raymond L. Reese.)

Index ❖

(Page numbers followed by " f " refer to footnotes.)

228

Additional copies of this book may be obtained
from your local bookstore,
or by sending $14.95 per paperback copy, postpaid,
or $20.95 per hardback copy, postpaid, to:

Hope Publishing House
P.O. Box 60008
Pasadena, CA 91116

California residents please add 8.5% sales tax
FAX orders to (818) 792-2121
Telephone VISA/MC orders to (800) 326-2671

Margaret Ainslie Fuad graduated from Lewis and Clark College with a B.A. degree and from San Francisco Theological Seminary with an M.A. degree in Missions and Christian Education.

Her energies for the past two decades have gone into promoting, organizing and educating toward prevention and treatment of alcoholism and other alcohol abuse problems within and outside the church. Besides chairing the committee which established the first recovery facility for alcoholics in her community, she has spearheaded the organization of the Presbyterian Alcohol Network (now the Presbyterian Network on Alcohol & Other Drug Abuse). In 1989 Ms. Fuad was honored by that organization which established an annual awards program bearing her name and which named her the first recipient of this award.

She lives with her husband in Visalia, California. They have one son and two grandchildren.